STAY CURIOUS

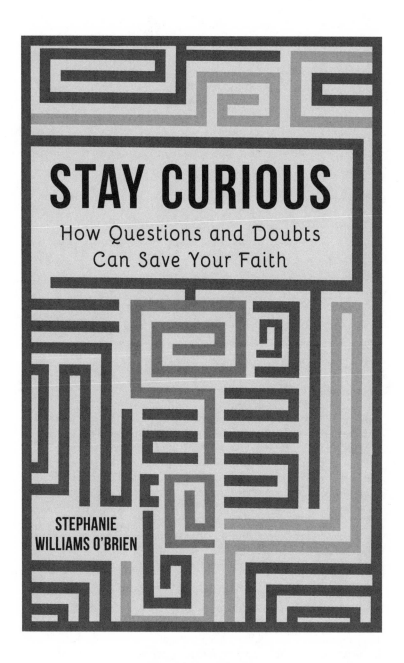

STAY CURIOUS

How Questions and Doubts Can Save Your Faith

STEPHANIE WILLIAMS O'BRIEN

Fortress Press

Minneapolis

STAY CURIOUS
How Questions and Doubts Can Save Your Faith

Published by Fortress Press, an imprint of 1517 Media, and in association
with the Books & Such Literary Management, 52 Mission Circle (Suite
122) PMB 170, Santa Rosa, CA 95409-5370, www.booksandsuch.com. All
rights reserved. Except for brief quotations in critical articles or reviews, no
part of this book may be reproduced in any manner without prior written
permission from the publisher. Email copyright@1517.media or write to
Permissions, Fortress Press, PO Box 1209, Minneapolis, MN 55440-1209.

Cover image: Shutterstock 2019; Abstract vector background design with
maze texture by SilverCircle
Cover design: Laura Drew

Print ISBN: 978-1-5064-4956-2
eBook ISBN: 978-1-5064-4957-9

The paper used in this publication meets the minimum requirements of
American National Standard for Information Sciences — Permanence of
Paper for Printed Library Materials, ANSI Z329.48-1984.

Manufactured in the U.S.A.

To my husband, JD, and my nephew, Amos.
Two of the most curious people I know and love.

TABLE OF CONTENTS

Part 3: How to Stay Curious: A Life of Passionate Uncertainty   237

PART 1

Wandering to
Wondering

Choosing Disruption

Without disruptions in life,
where would we be?
—Sarah Gadon

I couldn't pray, I couldn't worship.

I couldn't sit through another Bible study where another person's pain or joy was met with responses right out of the religious section of a greeting-card display.

"God has everything in control."

"When God closes a door, he opens a window."

"God took your loved one because he needed another angel."

I just couldn't do it. My own questions and doubts had brought me to a place where I could no longer go through the motions. I hadn't anticipated how hard it would be to trust God as I watched my dad take his last breath my senior year of high school. I didn't realize how hard it would be to encounter so many new ideas and perspectives when I went off to college. I couldn't believe that I was only in my twenties and already facing chronic pain from sports injuries and unexplained headaches. I was filled with questions that overwhelmed me on a daily basis:

How do I pray to a God who seems distant?

What do the ancient stories in the Bible have to do with my life today?

How do I deal with the reality that my beliefs have shifted?

What do I do about no longer feeling at home in the faith community I was raised in?

Why do politics seem to dictate the expressions of faith I see around me?

What does God think of my friends who are good people but don't follow Jesus?

How can I be a part of a group that has so many people who seem to do the opposite of what Jesus stood for but still do it in his name?

How do I trust a Being who allows hatred, violence, and injustice to exist in our world?

How do I process the anger I have toward what I see happening in the world?

What do I do about the contempt I am beginning to feel for other Christians who seem to not care for the poor or about racism or the marginalized? Were they reading the same Bible I felt obligated to read most of my life?

What if the God I thought I believed in doesn't exist at all?

I was stuck. The questions I had, and the inability of my community to hold them, made me feel like I was standing in quicksand up to my waist.

This is the story of how I managed to get free from the quicksand, one inch at a time. How I stopped looking at questions and doubts as holding me back, and how I stepped into a life where questions led to new experiences and discoveries. This is the story about how I reclaimed curiosity and chose a life of passionate uncertainty. About how I began to embrace questions and doubts—and how it saved my faith.

I emerged from the quicksand with a deeper understanding of myself and those around me. I learned more than I ever thought I could about life and the pursuit of meaning and purpose. I was set free to live into a more vibrant understanding of God and what it means to be a person who truly follows Jesus. This is the story of how I decided to stay curious and why I'll never go back to a life without questions.

This isn't just my story, this is *our* story. We are created to be curious—to wonder, to discover, to question, and yes, to doubt. Curiosity is a key part of what it means to be human. We have the cognitive ability to think beyond our immediate surroundings. It's what separates us from the other mammals on the planet. We each get to choose whether to embrace curiosity or ignore and suppress it.

For many of us who grew up in religious environments, our surroundings have thrust us toward the latter. The curiosity we were born with, and engaged with easily in our childhood, is snuffed out by the expectations placed upon us as we come of age. As we step into the constructs formed by the cultures around us, our curiosity is squelched.

As a Christian growing up in the church in North America, I've noticed that these constructs are impressed upon us at an early age. My childhood experience with church culture was highly structured, and I was encouraged to memorize answers, not ask questions. The adults in my life shared with me their understanding of what it meant to be a Jesus follower—and I know they meant well. But as I entered adulthood, the suppression of my inquisitiveness had taken a significant toll on my ability to ask questions about God, faith, and the church. I had been stripped of my curiosity.

Perhaps you feel like you are wandering, confused by what seems like a wilderness—like you are stuck in the same quicksand I was. You might feel like the faith system you'd come to trust is now more like a fortress trapping you inside. Maybe you're reading this, and the first thing you notice is the *lack* of questions you have about your faith. Curiosity and wonder could bring a new and meaningful dynamic to your life of faith. It may mean the important decision to choose curiosity over comfort.

It is time for all of us to embrace curiosity and disrupt the status quo. Disruption often has negative connotations—someone disrupted a meeting, or the Wi-Fi is out and it disrupted our screen time. However, disruption has significant benefits. Without disruption in the transportation industry, we'd only have horse-drawn carriages. Without disruption to the communication and technology world, we'd still be rewinding answering machines and video tapes from Blockbuster. Sometimes, we must choose to let our life be disrupted, or we will never grow or be set free.

We Believe in Believing

I sat down to coffee with a friend and mentor of mine recently. Rod is one of my curiosity heroes. He asks questions with such passion and integrity that I envy the words as soon as they come out of his mouth. His favorite questions to ask usually start with "Help me understand . . ." and then he expresses something he's noticed about my life or actions. Rod's incredible ability to understand people has helped me discover new things about myself.

"How did you become such a curious person?" I asked him. He explained that he had a lot to overcome before he was able to live a life of curiosity.

"I grew up in a home in the Bible Belt. The motto in our family was 'we believe in believing' and that was that," Rod told me. But, even as a child, he sensed there had to be something more, so he pushed through the environment of well-meaning pastor types and dug deeper into the inquiries rather than running from them.

In many ways, I was just like Rod as a child. It never went well when someone gave me an instruction. I would ask why I had to follow along, and they would say

Because I said so.

That's just the way it is.

You'll understand when you're older.

It's okay if it doesn't make sense; just have a little more faith.

As a little girl growing up in the church, these phrases bounced off me like the twenty-five-cent super-bouncy balls I'd beg my mom to buy me at the mall. The statements rang with dissonance, and I saw right through their flimsy logic. I have always had questions. Even as a child, I was never one to accept a basic answer or a simplified rebuttal. I was that kid always asking, "why?"

It seemed like the adults around me couldn't handle what my young mind was processing. They hoped a felt-board story line or a cheesy VeggieTales movie would help me move along in my understanding of God. When a cucumber and a tomato are explaining the deepest questions of faith, you can see where the mystery of the God of the universe may get lost along the way.

Now as an adult, I understand the deep annoyance caused by my constant questioning. Like the drip of a leaky faucet, "why?" seems fine at first, but as it keeps going, you reach a point where you swear you will lose your mind if you hear it once more. Now I sometimes wish for some animated fruits or vegetables to provide some answers every once in a while so I can take a break! But my nephew is in that phase right now, and when he asks "why?" I often respond, "that is a really good question buddy." Then we work together to find out, usually with the help of Google or Siri on my iPhone. It's in those moments I wonder what we miss out on by squelching the curiosity of the kids in our lives.

Most kids grow out of their questioning. They begin to feel as though the answers the world offers will suffice. They begin to trust those who "say so"—those with titles, experience, and research.

Still others, not satisfied with the pat answers offered by their environment, search for more. Many come up empty, finding only a vague void after the answers of those who "say so" fall short. They begin to wander with a growing sense they've lost their way.

When People *Should* on You

Like most people, I grew out of my nagging obsession with asking "why." I'm disturbed by how I also seemed to grow out of the ability to truly be curious. Perhaps it wasn't so much that I grew out of it, but my surroundings suggested that I *should*. I *should* receive the answers given to me and step forward without snagging the fabric of my community by asking more questions, thus pulling on a thread that might cause the tapestry created for me to unravel. I have memories of being asked to stay back after Sunday school and being told I *should* stay quiet and not ask so many questions because they were disrupting the class. I wasn't the kind of kid who brushed it off when I got in trouble; I really wanted to please the adults around me. This all fueled the fear I had that questions were somehow wrong, inappropriate, or maybe even dangerous.

Should is a powerful word. It suggests expectations that we put on ourselves or that are put on us by others. When we *should* on ourselves, or let others *should* on us, nothing good results. It's usually a mess.

I have been able to reclaim curiosity one question at a time. Questions that had plagued me became the chisel that chipped away at the brick tower of truths that I thought my life should be built upon.

Curiosity didn't kill me; it rescued me.

But fear of asking too many questions nearly held me back, keeping me captive to the purposeless fortress that had been built around my life. It can be especially pronounced in the church and among followers of Jesus. Nearly every question seems to be met with a reflexive answer before the question has even been fully formed. It's a carefully constructed catechism, ready at the tip of the tongue to squelch the curiosity, and potential doubt, of the questioner.

It's as though the most important quest of the Jesus follower is to have a succinct response to all of life's questions. This seems like an interesting goal for a group of people who follow a man who rarely had a simple or concise response when questions were asked of him.

It's not that people didn't bring their questions to Jesus; it's just that his typical response to questioners was to offer an additional question. Other times he just told mysterious and often scandalous stories. I can't understand why those who bear the name of Christ prefer fixed precepts rather than the bewildering stories Jesus so clearly preferred.

There is another way. A deeper way. An even more exciting way to live!

Jesus's life offers some invitations to ask questions that can change our lives—maybe even questions that could change the world.

In this book we will *wonder* together. Questions, and even doubts, can push us deeper into a faith we can actually trust in rather than further from a God we think we can contain. We will explore the obstacles that might keep us from stepping into curiosity. Finally, I will urge you to choose to reclaim curiosity in your life and take the steps to get there.

Together we can explore the idea that, perhaps, not all who *wonder* are lost.

A Catechism of Curiosity

cat·e·chism 'kadə͵kizəm/ *noun*

- *A summary of the principles of Christian religion in the form of questions and answers, used for the instruction of Christians.*
- *A series of fixed questions, answers, or precepts used for instruction in other situations.*[1]

I remember spending an exorbitant amount of time as a child having to memorize things: multiplication tables, states, countries, presidents, driver's-ed rules, the periodic table of elements, algebra equations, the list could go on. I look back and realize what I actually learned was how to memorize things quickly, rather than how to learn things I could retain long term.

My experience in Christian education was no exception. I found myself having to memorize Bible verses, the correct order of the sixty-six books of the Bible, and the names of the disciples. Not to mention all the words to the church musicals I was in every spring. Said musical usually included a large costumed character that was some sort of combination of a spiritual guide and a small-town high-school mascot. I admit, the idea of a singing songbook or a computer that talked and skated around on rollerblades really drew me in as a kid.

I'll also be honest and say that memorizing all those Bible verses has been beneficial in my life as an adult, and not just because I'm a pastor. A verse or phrase often comes to mind in moments that feel deep with meaning and purpose, and I find that much more rewarding than the candy I earned for memorizing those verses originally. When I've experienced loss and pain, Scriptures that help remind me God is with me have been a lifeline.

Even so, the obligation to memorize so much in so many areas of life was constant. I was also required to memorize statements of belief, taken from the catechism of my faith tradition. Many, if not most, Christian traditions have some form of catechism, which is a series of fixed questions, answers, or precepts used for instruction. In my denomination, or brand of Christian church, we were asked to memorize twenty-six statements of belief as part of our Christian education program in middle school called confirmation class—a three-year weekly class where we could "confirm" for ourselves what had been chosen for us by our parents as small children.

The word *catechism* first appeared in church writings in the Middle Ages, but the concept of catechism dates back to some of the earliest days of the church. Early Christians were taught the important beliefs of Christianity in a class or experience called *Catechesis*. Now, this kind of instruction more often takes place in what we call confirmation class, Sunday school, or Christian education classes. The etymology of the word comes from the Greek word *katekhizein*, which means *oral instruction*.

Catholics and Protestants both have a form of catechism, even if that word is not used to describe their lists of questions and answers. The current *Catechism of the Catholic Church* is a 755-page book with 2,865 catechism statements or paragraphs. This large collection was first brought together by Pope John Paul II in 1992, following a six-year process of writing and gathering its contents by twelve cardinals and bishops (the highest leadership roles in the Catholic Church). Martin Luther, at the onset of the Reformation, transformed the catechism into more of a question-and-answer format.

As a pastor, I can see why breaking down a Christian worldview into short statements can be helpful—especially when people are in certain stages of their faith. I lead a church of individuals who find themselves all over the map of their faith journey. So I know firsthand how complicated it can be to create a space for people to learn and question.

So as a teenager in confirmation, I was responsible for memorizing these questions and the one-sentence answers that my tradition had deemed important for our adolescent minds to store. While I think their intentions were good, I now look back and wonder what it suggested to me as a young person to think you can answer questions like, "what is salvation?" and "what is the Christian hope?" in one sentence.

One sentence.

Who is God? God is personal, eternal Spirit, Creator of the universe, Father of our Lord Jesus Christ, and our Father.

What is sin? Sin is all in thought, word, and deed that is contrary to the will of God.

What is salvation? Salvation is the work of God through Christ by which God forgives us our sin, frees us from guilt, and restores us to a right relationship with God.

Don't get me wrong, I was happy they were so short, but only because I had to memorize every word. In the midst of these twenty-six questions are some of the most important questions to ask about God, life, and humanity.

Other catechism questions: What does it mean to be a human being? What is God's relationship to the world? What is the kingdom of God? What is the purpose of the church?

Important questions, right?

Sure, it was easier to memorize one sentence, but I was also subtly and insidiously shaped by the way each response was so fixed and concise. I was being formed into someone who thought these answers were set and that curiosity was not needed to explain an infinite God. The God contained in the catechism eventually became a God I no longer wanted to follow, much less believe in. You might feel resistance to my suggestion that these statements limit our understanding of God. A shift to thinking of God outside the boundaries created by these short sentences could expand your mind and heart toward the depth and breadth of an infinite God.

In the 755-page *Catechism of the Catholic Church*, there is an entire section devoted to the "mystery of God." What if the catechism of our faith was that we were given permission to explore the mystery of God? What if leaders of churches, like me, responded to questions with even more questions, just like Jesus did? What if our catechism, our "oral instruction," was to say, "Keep going! Keep asking! Keep exploring! Keep wondering!"?

Our faith will be radically more alive if we create a catechism of curiosity rather than a catechism of certainty.

The Question Man

Jesus never answered questions with a catechism response.

If you read the story of Jesus's life as told in the four Gospels, you get the impression that this man would never lead a class with a predefined question-and-answer format. Nowhere can I find an example of Jesus responding to a question with what could be considered a catechism response. This man, who many consider God in the flesh, is not an answer man.

He's a question man.

In Mark's version of Jesus's story, one day Jesus is in the temple courts, walking confidently into a religious environment that he often prophetically challenges. Some of the religious leaders, teachers, and elders come up to him and ask him what seems like a simple question. They have seen him turn tables in the temple, heal the sick in the streets, and offer the forgiveness of sins to those who don't seem to deserve it.

"By what authority are you doing these things?" they ask.

Jesus replies, "I will ask you one question. Answer me, and I will tell you by what authority I am doing these things. John's baptism—was it from heaven or of human origin? Tell me!"

The leaders discuss among themselves, knowing that either way they respond, they will end up looking bad in front of those in the Jewish community whose respect they want to keep. So they tell him they don't know.

Jesus tells them that if they won't answer him, then he won't answer their question either. Mark's version of the story says that "Jesus then began to speak to them in parables."[2] Jesus goes on to tell them a story that they do not appreciate, and it results in confusion and outrage. It's here that these leaders begin the plan to have Jesus arrested and killed.

Arrested because he wouldn't answer their question. Killed on account of his failure to answer with the proper statement of belief. He wouldn't tell them what they wanted to hear, and that fueled their anger. Not all of those who asked Jesus questions were trying to trap him in his words. Many characters in this ancient story display the kind of curiosity I'm suggesting we should pursue.

Another religious leader, Nicodemus, comes to Jesus with his questions. Jesus responds with what seems like a radical metaphor about being born again. And Jesus offers questions back, which engage Nicodemus's heart and mind so much that by the time Jesus is killed, Nicodemus is willing to follow him even if it costs him his reputation and potentially life.[3]

Then there is the woman doing her daily task of drawing water up from a well. Jesus asks her to give him some water. She is curious and asks why he spoke to her since her gender and ethnicity normally would have precluded a rabbi, a male Jewish leader, from engaging with her in public. Question after question she asks him. Jesus answers with a beautiful, yet mysterious word picture about water that can quench her thirst for good. After their conversation, this woman runs through her community with yet another question on her mind, "Could this man be the Messiah? The Savior they had all been waiting for?"[4]

The disciples, those closest to Jesus and his first followers, ask Jesus questions all the time. Much to their frustration, he never offers succinct or condensed answers.

One day, Jesus teaches a group of people near a lake, telling stories and parables to illustrate how his kingdom is different. There are so many people that he has to sit in a boat out in the water. Later, his disciples ask him questions about all the stories he told that day.

Jesus responds to their questions by saying, "The secret of the kingdom of God has been given to you. But to those on the outside everything is said in parables so that they may be ever seeing but never perceiving, and ever hearing but never understanding; otherwise they might turn and be forgiven!"[5]

What? How confusing! This response begs *so many more* questions. Jesus is quoting a part of the Hebrew Scriptures where God speaks through the prophet Isaiah. And while the quote gives us some context for Jesus's response, its meaning still isn't entirely clear.

And just as quickly as he finishes explaining the parable he just told, Jesus jumps into three more parables about what the kingdom of God is like. The guy didn't seem to have a problem coming up with metaphors and stringing them together in a monologue.

Jesus invites us to step into the mystery of who he is and what the kingdom of God is all about. He doesn't even hint at the idea that questions are off limits; he welcomes them and offers more. Jesus's life suggests that God isn't as interested in the right answers so much as the right questions. The inability to fully comprehend who God is seems to invite wonder, not closure.

When we get our hearts set on having all the right answers, on escaping the tension of following a God who is bigger than our finite minds can hold, we trap ourselves in the *need* for answers. We seek a clarity that perhaps God never intended for us to have.

If Jesus offered a catechism in response to questions, his questioners could go on their way and decide if the simple answer would suffice—or not. And this still happens today. Many people are walking away from the church feeling like oversimplified answers don't work in the real world. I don't blame them!

Curiosity in Community

God wants more than robots who can spout programmed answers. I'd even go so far as to say that God prefers the doubting cynic who is constantly peppering God with questions than a content, yet disconnected person going through the motions.[6] When we see God's goal as relationship, not rhetoric, we begin to see why our catechism must be one of curiosity if we have any hope of joining a God who still moves in the world.

When we find ourselves waist deep in the quicksand of our questions, it can be tempting to try to escape—to set all of our questions aside just to avoid the quicksand altogether.

I went to a Christian college where I wrestled with doubt more than I ever had up until that point in my life. I sat in classes and felt like I couldn't just accept what was being taught by my professors. Was everyone else able to take notes and accept what was written on these clip-art laden PowerPoint presentations? At times I wanted to run, but I knew the questions would be right on my heels. I couldn't run fast enough to escape my own mind and heart.

You may look around a Sunday-school class, small group, sermon series, or even your family and think you are the only one asking questions, the only one full of doubts. It is tempting to think that those who are not questioning are missing something and are behind in some way.

The truth is, you aren't the only one. Many, if not most, people of faith encounter doubts and questions throughout their life, and not everyone is in the same faith stage at the same time. This doesn't mean you're ahead of someone else in some sort of race. It's not a competition. There is no finish line to cross or medal to be won. No one will get a prize or a consolation trophy for just showing up to the event. Spiritual elitism is not a healthy response to the awakening you're experiencing as you go deeper in your curiosity.

Everyone is on their own road. This can be difficult in a community, especially when it is hard to tell who else is asking the same questions as you. And it can be even more difficult in a marriage or close friendship when you have to acknowledge faith exploration doesn't happen the same way for you as it does for your loved one.

I have often discovered that my close friends or ministry partners were in different places in their faith while we tried to stay relationally connected. Only when I could give them space to engage God in their own way and on their own time could I be set free to do the same. In the long run, we'd both grow in our understanding and pursuit of curiosity as well as in our relationship with each other. It turns out, curiosity can also bring people together if we handle each other's questions with care and step toward questions together rather than run from them.

The problem with wanting to run from our questions is that the lack of answers can cause an existential crisis. If in the meantime we have also run from community, we can end up in a difficult place. Whether it is the end of a relationship, the inability to conceive, mental or physical illness, or the loss of a needed job, when life hits you, the unanswered questions follow closely behind like a one-two punch to the gut. These life circumstances are difficult to face no matter what, and doing so alone can be unbearable.

But even questions that seem to lead to a dead end or answers that never suffice don't have to leave us in confusion.

Questions Are Powerful

Psychologists and counselors teach us that questions don't merely lead to new knowledge. Questions are generative. They generate new experiences, foster new ideas and innovations, and help us engage resources we didn't realize were right under our noses. Questions lead to deeper relationships with God and others. They create platforms for change and transformation in our lives and in our communities. *Quest* is literally the way the word begins. It's no wonder a good question will take you on a journey.

Thinking of questions this way reveals why God invites us to wonder: so that we can move forward in the *quest* to be fully alive. It also reveals why many people experience faith as stale, boring, and confining. When we cease to ask questions, curiosity comes to a halt.

You can trade *wandering* for an intentional pursuit of *wonder*. As you engage with your questions, they will generate new ideas and experiences. If we are following the "question man," perhaps we can become "question people" and allow a sense of intrigue to guide us into a depth of meaning in our life we have not yet experienced.

Not All Who *Wonder* Are Lost

Always be on the lookout for
the presence of wonder.
—E. B. White

You might have seen the bumper sticker "Not all who wan-der are lost" proudly displayed on anything from a beat-up old Jeep to a Prius Hybrid. When I see it, a smile always creeps across my face. I assume the driver is a Lord of the Rings fan and probably doesn't feel controlled by a map or obsessed with a destination. When I think about it, I long to take off in any direction and find whatever I might discover along the path.

The problem is that wandering in real life usually doesn't feel like an adventure. It feels like the wilderness—full of unknown dangers. Wandering through a wilderness, with no apparent exit, often feels like a nightmare.

Pressing into new ways of thinking can be exciting at first—like a whole new world is opening up. But for most of us, any thrill from new ideas and perspectives is quickly squelched by the weight of the questions and doubts that arise. The wilderness feels completely foreign, a terrain we are ill equipped to navigate. We look at the wilderness that surrounds us and realize we can journey in any direction, and the truth is, we have no idea where we will end up.

Let me tell you about Sam. He found himself in the wilderness unexpectedly after a broken relationship and some bad experiences with a few Christians who, let's just say, weren't exactly following the heart of Jesus. This season of questions came during the peak of the popularity of the young-adult dystopian novel-turned-film *The Hunger Games*. So Sam felt like one of those futuristic hovercrafts had dropped him into the woods without anything to defend himself with.

He felt like he was plopped down right in the middle of a forest so thick with trees that only glimmers of light could get in. He couldn't tell which way would lead him out of the darkness and doubt, but he knew he had to do something.

He tried to find books, films, and podcasts that addressed the questions consuming his mind. Sometimes he'd fall down an online rabbit hole so deep that before he knew it, it was 2:00 a.m., only a few hours before he had to be up for work. Thoughts constantly buzzed in his mind, especially when someone was talking about faith or the Divine. He found it difficult to quiet the noise when he needed to go to sleep or pay attention in a meeting at work, so he turned to hours of mind-numbing video games and nights out with friends who were also trying to numb their own pain and worry. He could escape from the darkness for a time, but it was always short-lived.

Not knowing how to take intentional steps in any direction, Sam began to wander, feeling lost without a compass. There was none of the excitement or whimsy the bumper sticker implied, just a sense of dread. He eventually found himself in what felt like the quicksand I had experienced—stuck. Those pits can come up unexpectedly in unknown terrain. Questioning became wandering, and wandering led to being stuck.

Wilderness Seasons of Life

We all experience wilderness in our lives—it's not a matter of if but when we will find ourselves in a period of wilderness wandering. For most people, wilderness seasons are cyclical and happen throughout our lives when we experience questions, doubts, loss, transition, or other disruptions.

The theme of wilderness crops up all over the place in the narrative of the Bible—from the forty years the Israelites spent wandering in the desert in Exodus to the forty days Jesus spent in the wilderness in preparation for ministry. All of these wilderness accounts share one thing in common: the storyteller believes that it is God who leads the people into the wilderness.

> God led the people around by the desert road toward the Red Sea. (Exodus 13:18 NIV)

> Therefore I [God] led them out of Egypt and brought them into the wilderness. (Ezekiel 20:10 NIV)

> Then Jesus was led by the Spirit into the wilderness. (Matthew 4:1 NIV)

Why would God lead people, who God supposedly *loved*, into such treacherous and difficult conditions?

Having the benefit of hindsight, we can see that wilderness leads to something better, something greater, something more that God wanted for them. In the story of the exodus, the people were in captivity. They had much more certainty than they did in the wilderness, but they weren't free. Sometimes what seems like certainty in our lives is actually just a form of sneaky bondage. God wants us to be able to live freely!

In each story, when the people are in the middle of the wilderness, uncertainty is towering around them. The questions and doubts feel all-consuming: Will we have our needs met?

Is God really there? Should we find other gods? How can we trust this God who is leading us into the wilderness? Maybe we should just go back to where we came from; even though we weren't free, at least we knew what to expect.

But they couldn't go back. Once you're in the wilderness, you have now seen too much. Going back to where you started isn't an option.

Uncertainty often clouds the views of those in the story. But there is something at the other end that God deeply wants for those being led through the wilderness: a life that is more free, full, and vibrant than anything they could have experienced without the journey through the woods.

There's no way to know for certain whether it is God leading you away from a place of comfort and into a place of wilderness. If it *is* God leading you, it could mean there is something significant worth pursuing on the other side of the forest, desert, or woods (with some experience, I have found that the wilderness can take many forms in different seasons of life). You might feel like you want to turn around and go back. I know I did! The tension of the wilderness strains your mind and heart, and it's exhausting.

If, like me, you found yourself stuck in the quicksand of doubt, questions, and confusion, perhaps you don't have to stay there. You can't go back to where you came from, but maybe you don't have to wander in the wilderness of uncertainty alone.

What if *wonder* is the point of the wilderness?

Wandering versus Wondering

If the wilderness wandering we read about in Scripture were reframed as a time of wonder, it would be an entirely different experience! I see the difference between *wandering* and *wondering* like this:

Wandering is a coping mechanism of avoidance that tries to minimize what is uncomfortable.

Wondering is an active pursuit of questions and a willingness to risk the tension in the unknown.

Wandering is a way to steer clear of the stress that comes from a deep concern about the direction that might be best for you and others around you.

Wondering is a heightened curiosity about God, yourself, others, and the world that, while often uncomfortable, is full of passion and intrigue.

Wandering is motivated by fear, confusion, apathy, and an endless search for novelty.

Wondering is motivated by passionate uncertainty about the mystery of God and the excitement that comes with discovery.

Throughout the story, God was inviting a different approach. And God still offers that invitation to us—to take on a posture of wonder.

Wonder that fuels our passion and leads to discovery. Wonder that pushes us to even deeper questions and away from pat answers. God is calling us not to satisfying contentment but to deeper meaning-making experiences—the kind of experiences that bring a community or a family closer together rather than further apart. The kind of journey that invites the courage to risk and squelches apathy.

With questions propelling us along the way, we *wonder* through the woods rather than wander.

Those who wonder aren't lost—they are propelled by curiosity. They may not know the destination, but learning and discovery begin to mean more.

Let's get back to Sam's story. I should tell you that Sam is a stand-in for all kinds of people I've encountered in my life. Maybe you see some of Sam's story in your own. Perhaps you've tried different methods of plowing through or escaping the wilderness, but the core realities of the wilderness resonate with some of your experience.

So the end of Sam's story depends on the choice between wandering and wondering. There are as many different results as there are stories, but I see two overarching themes.

The Sams who continue to wander often have an increase in frustration, apathy, anger, and general dissatisfaction in their life. I see many of them end up isolated from others, including their faith communities, families, and sometimes even their spouses or former confidants. They grow frustrated that everyone around them doesn't seem to "get it" and struggle to see why others aren't also wandering through the wilderness. Some of these Sams conclude that others simply aren't as enlightened, and they begin to disconnect from people and communities. On their own, they begin to lose their passion for justice or causes they once cared about. Wandering has kept them from being propelled by the purpose that used to guide them. Even the spiritual practices that had been helpful are set aside as the distractions of daily life take over.

Then there are the Sams who begin to let the wonder of their questions lead them through the trees and out of what once seemed like perpetual darkness. Their destination is unknown, but as they journey through the wilderness, they find themselves glimpsing what Oliver Wendell Holmes Jr. once called "the far side of complexity." The questions aren't all answered, but they don't loom like they once did. These Sams are able to participate communally again, but now in ways that are fresh with meaning and a deeper understanding of the world around them. Having been through it, they have a lot more grace than they once did for others who might think differently.

They know that they need others to understand God and themselves. Ultimately, they have made the personal choice to *actively integrate* their faith with their life experiences. They probably have a very different understanding of God than they had before the wilderness, but they have peace with the continual process of knowing God. It's a reality that some come to a place where they don't believe God exists and start to experience how much faith is required for that conclusion. Those who have taken responsibility for their faith formation realize their own agency in the decisions they make to live that faith out in the world. The distinction is, they didn't get to where they are by accident, but rather guided by *wonder.*

The far side of complexity is not something easily reached; it's not a destination of certainty that we may hope for. By taking it one step at a time, propelled by wonder through the wilderness seasons of life, we all can experience the freedom that comes when we embrace wonder.

Two very different outcomes, but it starts with one choice. To wander or to wonder.

The History of Mystery

*I have come to love the darkness—
for I believe now that it is part of
a very, very small part of Jesus'
darkness and pain on earth.*
—Mother Teresa[1]

We sat in the car in the driveway of my sister-in-law Claire's house talking for a while before we finally realized we'd been burning too much gas to keep the heat on and it was time to finish our Minnesota goodbye. In Minnesota, where I'm from, we call a goodbye that goes on and on a *Minnesota goodbye* because they are so common here. This time, it wasn't because we had more family gossip to catch up on or funny stories to tell about my niece and nephew. It was one of those "the conversation just got real deep right before we had reached our destination" experiences.

Claire had been relatively open with me about the struggles she was having as she tried to relate to God and the church. Often, when you are in a time of deconstruction in your faith, it's hard to put words to what you're going through emotionally and spiritually. But it proved to be important that she tried and didn't stay alone in her wrestling. She was full of questions, none with easy answers: "Maybe what I thought I had experienced with God in the past wasn't real? Maybe I need to try another expression of church? Maybe I have been avoiding the questions because I am afraid of the answers?"

She was getting to the core of what she feared. That if she moved any further into the questions, if she began to overturn the stones along the path, she'd discover that there was nothing beneath them. That her quest to find an authentic spirituality would hit a dead end with a door that opened to reveal that there was nothing there all along.

I listened and tried to ask some good clarifying questions. As one of the pastors at her current church, I shared what I knew to be true. "Trust me. You're not the only one who feels this way!" I exclaimed. An expression of doubt mixed with relief came over her face.

It's common to hold back and not reveal the depth of our searching and our doubts, and it's certainly rare for anyone to admit they are afraid. There are a lot of reasons that we find this difficult—particularly in forms of Christianity that don't cultivate a sense of mystery around God. But it hasn't always been that way, and I think things are beginning to change.

Looking Back in Order to Move Forward

If you walk through the musty rows of a library at a theological school or seminary, you will find many books that seem to have been left untouched for decades. In the section labeled Church History, you will likely find some of the dustiest books of them all. It's not always the most riveting subject.

The failure to truly look back so that we can move forward is a common human problem—not just for Christians. We often don't recognize that where we've come from has shaped who we are. The church, in particular, has quite a sordid history. You don't have to look too far to see the many groups of people who have been oppressed or even killed in the name of the God of the Bible.

Christians either tend to want to emphasize the glories of the church's past or dwell on the church's failures. The idea that history repeats itself is lauded by those hoping to return to the glory days and is suggested as a warning by those who understand that Christianity supported or undergirded tragedies like the Crusades and the Holocaust.

I tend to believe that history doesn't repeat itself but rather *echoes* itself. There is something familiar from the past that can echo into future generations. An echo from church history is reverberating louder and transcending our current divisions. That is the echo of the voices of the Christian mystics, whose main life pursuit was the *mystery of God*. In the lives of these Jesus followers and their writings and practices, we find a rich and deep history.

Mysticism is difficult to encapsulate in a sentence. But my best definition would be "a finite human being's intentional and relational pursuit of the mystery of the infinite reality of the Divine." Humans are finite and limited. God, by very definition, is infinite. So in order for a human to go deeper in relating to an infinite being, the human must surrender to the concept of mystery and accept the limitations of their finite human mind. By transcending the confines of logic, reason, and the pursuit of knowledge, we can experience God more fully.

Many Catholics and Protestants are returning to Christian mysticism as I define it here. An echo of the mystics of the past is pushing people to embrace centering prayer, intentional spiritual listening, and *lectio divina* (*divine listening* through meditating on Scripture). These practices are all ways to engage with the Divine and transcend our physical human experience, which is why we call them *spiritual* practices. To be clear, for anyone who is a little uneasy, Christian mysticism is not any of the following: fortune-telling, mind-reading, astrology, or new-age spirituality. It is an ancient spiritual practice that our ancestors in the faith passed down to us. I'm intentionally using the prefix *Christian* for the type of mysticism I describe here, although nearly every religion attempts to transcend the physical and engage the spiritual.

This rich history of the pursuit of the mystery of God should give us not only the permission to stay curious but perhaps even the motivation and vision for why questions are so vital to a vibrant faith. When the uncertain aspects of God feel like they are the most daunting, the stories of those who were often given the title of being a "mystic" might give us the will to go on!

Mysticism has a long history within Christianity, going back to ancient Jewish forms that predate Christianity. Even in the Bible, we see encounters with God that transcend finite human reality. The Torah, which is the Jewish name for the first five books of the Bible, recounts the history of God and God's people.

Genesis 12 describes the encounters between God and Abraham. Abraham must have had a mystical experience to believe that God was calling him to leave the land his family had lived on for generations to go to a new place. Unlike modern Western cultures, where young people can't wait to go off to college or travel to new parts of the world, people in the ancient world stayed in their homelands for generations. They didn't fill up their hatchback with all their material possessions and only return on holidays. Abraham's choice to move to a new land was unprecedented in many ways!

And from that point on, one mystical experience at a time, God's people were led by God's Spirit. Jacob experienced God through visions and dreams,[2] and he wrestled with God at the ford of the Jabbok River.[3] Moses talked with God through a burning bush.[4] The people of God followed a supernatural cloud.[5] The prophet Anna fasted and prayed in the temple for decades and got one glimpse of the infant Jesus. Words about him poured out from her heart to all those listening. I like to consider this the first sermon about the newborn king.[6] The stories of divine mystery go on and on. You can follow Jewish mysticism right up to some present-day rabbinic traditions.

The roots of Christian mysticism can perhaps be traced all the way back to the many mind-bending experiences the disciples had with Jesus during his ministry. They were full of questions for Jesus! But, as I said earlier, Jesus isn't an answer man but a question man. I would argue that Jesus was the father of Christian mysticism—deliberately ushering people into the mystery of God rather than giving succinct answers that would satisfy the curious. Jesus also engaged in the mystery as he mentioned the other members of the Trinity. Jesus described the Holy Spirit as a counselor and guide and referred to the additional person of the Trinity as Abba, an intimate, loving Father. At one point, when the Jewish religious leaders were trying yet again to trap him, Jesus responded with an interesting statement, "Very truly I tell you, the Son can do nothing by himself; he can do only what he sees his Father doing, because whatever the Father does the Son also does. For the

Father loves the Son and shows him all he does. Yes, and he will show him even greater works than these, so that you will be amazed."[7]

Jesus never described visibly seeing a physical manifestation of God the Father or the Holy Spirit. He was describing his ability to "see" what God the Father is doing and living into that reality in his human life on earth. I see this as inherently mystical, giving us a picture of how we too can attempt to discern what God is doing and join in.

The story of the early church, as told in the book of Acts, describes a whole slew of mysterious encounters with God. Pentecost is a paramount example: God's Spirit falls in such a powerful way that people begin to speak all sorts of languages.[8] Early church leaders like Peter, Paul, Lydia, and others rely on mystical experiences with God in which they have visions for guidance.[9] They describe trying to go to a certain town, but "the spirit of Jesus would not allow them to."[10] (I always wonder what exactly happened there. Was a hologram-like Jesus floating in the road blocking their way?) They say things like "it seemed good to the Holy Spirit and to us,"[11] as though the Holy Spirit was an *actual* dove sitting on someone's shoulder that they could just ask for directions.

From that point on, many in Christian history who pursued wonder and mystery as they sought God have been given the title of mystic: Origen of Alexandria, Augustine of Hippo, Catherine of Siena, Julian of Norwich, and many other modern mystics, including some alive today!

Your deep questions can move from something you avoid to a spirituality you put into practice. This was the next step for my sister-in-law, Claire. She started small with some spiritual practices that she hadn't tried before: forms of centering prayer and meditation with a focus on Jesus. She connected with a spiritual director, a person trained to listen spiritually as a coach and guide. My spiritual director has described their work as listening to me with one ear and the Holy Spirit with another.

Claire was beginning to pursue the mystery of God, breaking through the confining barriers and limitations that organized churches often cause. As someone who leads a church, I realize those limitations aren't usually created on purpose but are often a byproduct of the way we structure and define church experiences. How open to God's mystery can you be, spending an hour and fifteen minutes in a church building on Sundays? Claire's experience of God had to expand beyond only scheduled church activities and worship services. She learned to pursue the mystery of God as much as she had pursued her career and her vision for her family. She couldn't wait for the process to happen to her; she had to find the inner motivation to start and the resolve to sustain this intentional pursuit.

She had to be willing to be courageous in the face of fear and to begin to pursue her own faith, stepping one practice at a time into the unknown. This meant facing uncertainty in ways she had tried to avoid. She didn't know what she would find if she overturned the stones on her path, and nine years of wandering had taken their toll. So she mustered up the bit of wonder she could find and started to bravely choose to engage her curiosity and not hold it back any longer. She knew that she could live forever in fear of what she might discover if she were to truly ask the questions she was avoiding—that what she would find there would be a void, disproving her whole spiritual framework. But she finally realized that her curiosity outweighed her fear. At this point it would be better to just go for it and find out if her fears would be realized or if she would discover something more vibrant than before.

Engaging the mystery of God through spiritual practices is best done as an experiment. Give something a try for a season of time and see what the results are! A few months of trying out a practice regularly will give you a good idea of how helpful it may or may not be to you in your current season of life.

My go-to spiritual practices are from what is now referred to as *Ignatian spirituality*, spiritual practices developed by Saint Ignatius of Loyola, a sixteenth-century Spanish priest who founded the Jesuit Order, also known as the Society of Jesus. They are still one of the most influential orders in the Catholic Church today given their extensive work in education and social-justice ministries to the poor and those in need. A quick google search will result in numerous practices from Ignatius's collection, *The Spiritual Exercises*. If you are in a wilderness season of life, what experiment could you try that might help you become unstuck? If the results of the first experiment aren't great, try something else. The mystery of God has been pursued for thousands of years; take your time, give yourself grace, and learn something new. In part 2 of this book, I will give you some ideas of experiments you can try.

Step by step, Claire began to overcome the fear she had been facing for almost a decade. It didn't happen overnight, and it certainly wasn't easy, but she started to see glimpses of the far side of complexity, which had seemed impossible for so long. It was the beginning of the end of her "dark night of the soul"—which is how prominent Christian mystic Saint John of the Cross describes a long season where God feels absent. Even Mother Teresa experienced dark nights of the soul. I've found that most devout Jesus followers have.

Inspired by those who have come before us, we can step into greater wonder with our eyes wide open, ready for our minds to expand. I think it's about time Claire owns her rightful spot as a mystic—Claire of Minneapolis. Could you be next? Join my friends Keisha of Tampa, Laura of Columbia Heights, Matthew of Winnipeg, Heidi of Saint Paul, Steve of Maple Grove, and so many others whose main life pursuit is the *mystery of God*.

Praying to a God You Don't Believe In

*Those who believe that they believe in God,
but without passion in their hearts, without
anguish in mind, without uncertainty,
without doubt, without an element of
despair even in the consolation, believe
only in the God idea, not God Himself.*
—Miguel de Unamuno

I love to travel. When my feet have been on the ground too long, I begin to yearn for adventure. This means I end up spending a lot of time in airports. I've gotten pretty good at timing things right, arriving at the right time to get some coffee on the way to my gate, finding the best spots in airports to get some work done on layovers. But for some reason, I seem to constantly have what I call "TSA fails." Even after countless flights, I just can't seem to think through the things that cause a serious holdup with the Transportation Security Administration on my way in.

Somehow I wear the wrong outfit with the extra zippers, which results in an intimate, yet public experience with the TSA agent. I always think to myself that I need to empty my new Nalgene water bottle before I make it to the line, but alas, there goes another bottle along with whatever favorite stickers I had on it. One time I totally forgot that I had a whole container of peanut butter in my carry on.

One of my recent major TSA failures was heading to the airport in flip-flops because it was a hot summer day and realizing in line that many others in front of me also had sandals on. That meant I was going to have the unfortunate experience of walking through the x-ray machine barefoot and placing my feet on the yellow footprint outlines right where who *knows* how many potentially fungus-ridden feet had stepped!

As I was trying to think if there was any way I had a pair of socks in my computer bag, I noticed a young boy behind me, only four or five years old, messing around in line. He was darting in and out of the rope line, yelling and hollering at his little sister. His parents were visibly stressed, and I heard his dad say firmly, "Son, you better calm down or a mean man is going to come take you from us."

Without thinking, I audibly gasped. As I tried not to awkwardly stare at this family, out of the corner of my eye, I saw the look of sheer terror on this little boy's face. I think that his dad was trying to do the best he could in that moment; he was really stressed and probably concerned that there *would* be consequences for their family if he couldn't get his son under control. I have felt the burden of the kids under my care getting out of control—it's stressful for anyone!

When I saw the look on that little boy's face, I couldn't help but imagine this was an experience that would stick with him for a while. Trips to the airport were certainly going to be a different experience emotionally for this little boy.

Early in our lives, we receive so many messages about who God is—sometimes directly spoken to us, sometimes indirectly expressed through our experiences. Our environment shapes us, just like walking through TSA can make us feel more anxious about the dangers in the world. Many of us form negative concepts of God, and we can unearth those images if we begin to think about them. Narratives are formed in our minds that sound much like that dad in the airport:

"You better stop behaving like that or God will punish you."

"God won't love you if you do this or that—or if you *don't* do this or that."

"Do you want God to be proud of you? Then you better check all the religious boxes."

Think for a minute about some of the earliest memories you have of God in your life. Who helped shape your understanding? What environments gave you a picture of God? When do you first remember trying to imagine the Divine?

Discovering Your God Concept

All of us have had understandings of God throughout our lives. Perhaps your earliest image of God is a positive one, but most people who do this exercise with me think back and remember a negative image of God, or *god-concept* (not to be confused with a *God-complex*—that's a different conversation, though probably worth having in an age where narcissism is prevalent).

Psychologist Ana-Maria Rizzuto has been credited with first using the phrase *god-concept* to mean whatever our mind is using to represent who God is and what our relationship to God is like.[1] Her studies and others suggest that children begin to have a god concept as early as two to three years old. Some studies have shown that even kids who don't grow up in a religious environment develop a concept of a divine being that is bigger than them and transcends their internal and external worlds.

So every one of us has been trying to wrap our human finite mind around an infinite God for our whole life. Perhaps at times it was intentional on our part, or on the part of our caregivers, relatives, churches, or community groups. But even if it wasn't intentional, it has been happening. A god concept has been developing consciously and subconsciously through our relationships and experiences.

As an adult, you now have significant agency about your concept of God and about which experiences you'll engage in to form it. What will inform the pursuit of your image of God? Because God is infinite, the mystery of God can be explored but never conquered, so the journey toward your god concept is never ending. It is important to remember that your pursuit of God ventures beyond yourself. You have loved ones, a partner, perhaps kids, and together you will need to ask, How are *we* forming our continued understanding of the Divine?

Your concept of God is continually being formed, whether you are being intentional or not. Indecision is still a decision. There really is no neutral. Your life is moving forward. Your mind, and I'd suggest your soul, are forming concepts about who God is and who God isn't. And those concepts will have ramifications on how you live your life: what you do with your time, how you spend your energy, what you value enough to support with your time or money.

So it becomes crucial to try to understand what your current god concept is. Curiosity can lead you to intentional steps that form your understanding of *who* exactly you are praying to. What kind of God do you think is on the other end of your prayers?

When I began to explore my own concept of God more intentionally, I realized that I was praying to a god that I didn't really believe in. The image of God in my mind was a god who was peering down at the earth with a giant thumb ready to squash me like a bug if I made the wrong move. My unintentional god concept was not the God I actually experienced once I was curious enough to pay attention.

Sometimes people ask themselves, "Do I actually believe in God?" That can be a deep, life-defining question. However, a better first question could be: "Do I believe in the God of my current god concept?" The answer to that question could lead down a very different road.

When I ask people about their god concept and they reveal a deeply judgmental, angry, competitive God, I have to be honest with them and say, "If that image is who God is, then I'd choose atheism." I'm not advocating that we imagine God to be whoever we might want God to be. That's not a helpful approach either. It seems that there are two ditches we can fall into: (1) simply accepting whatever our life experiences, relationships, and surroundings have told us about who God is. Or (2) deciding to make God into whatever concept we'd prefer. Those who fall into the second ditch, interestingly enough, tend to imagine a God in their own image. Rizzuto calls this "the god in the mirror."[2]

Staying on the Road

If you want to stay on the road, and out of those two ditches, you have to take the steering wheel from whoever or whatever has been driving this god-concept vehicle in your life. Or perhaps no one has been driving! In either case, now is the time to take the wheel.

Grabbing the wheel is the first step on the road of intentionality when it comes to your concept of God. Human beings are complex, and we discover who God is through multiple avenues. As a person, and as a pastor, I can't deny that the Bible is an important and central source for developing a more accurate god concept. I'll dig into the concept of wrestling with the Bible more in part 2, but let me start here: I believe God gave the Bible to us not as a handbook for life but as a resource for knowing God more fully. This ancient collection of narratives, poems, and proverbs can't be distilled down to a simple set of rules.

A better approach would be to see the Bible as a collection of ancient stories, letters, and poetry about Yahweh (God). The supporting characters in the Bible are human beings attempting to respond to this God who is always reaching out to them, starting with the very act of creation. The humans never respond to God perfectly—most of the time they fail miserably—but the story suggests that God comes back to the failing humans again and again. Since God gave the humans the free will to respond however they want, God doesn't always protect them from every individual consequence to their choices. This ultimately wouldn't help them. It's just like when we don't protect our own kids from every not-so-great decision they make. It helps them learn!

By the end of the story, the Trinitarian God comes to earth in the form of Jesus, providing victory over the eternal consequences of being humans who often don't get it right. Jesus conquers the brokenness that separates humans from God by conquering death on the cross and coming back to life. This means there can be full reconciliation with God because the barriers have been removed.[3] There are many other ancient Near Eastern narratives about gods that the original audiences of the biblical books would have heard about or believed in. However, there is no other story where a god acts primarily out of love for humans rather than out of contempt, anger, or selfishness. In many narratives, the gods are depicted as generally being bothered by the very existence of humans rather than desperately wanting to be in relationship with humans and going to the greatest lengths to prove that core desire. The story about Yahweh in the Bible would have been a stark contrast to the narratives and worldview of that day. The Bible brought to light the god concepts of those original hearers of our ancient Scriptures, and I think it can do the same for us today.

In seasons of deconstruction, when you are picking apart your god concept to see what has developed, the Bible might be a core source of doubt and questions. It is absolutely worth exploring what this ancient book really means to you. If you feel like you need permission to question the Bible—to figure out if it really should be a part of how you develop your god concept—then you have it! I don't think you need a pastor's permission to take on that quest, but if you do, consider your permission slip signed. I encourage you to really go there, realize how many different ways of interpreting the Bible there are, and beware of falling back into the ditch of simply accepting the first perspective that seems intriguing so as to avoid having to think critically on a personal level. More on our approach to Scripture in part 2!

What Else Informs Our God Concept?

The Bible is by no means the only way we can understand God. *Sola scriptura* (by Scripture alone) is a central belief for many Christians. This doctrine, so to speak, simply means that no other original writings or words from certain leaders should be taken as having ultimate authority. For instance, we have writings from a man named Josephus, a historian from the first century who wrote about the culture in Rome around the same time that the Bible was compiled. Most Bible scholars take the writings of Josephus seriously, as they provide perspective about the ancient world. But that doesn't mean his writings are seen as having spiritual authority in our lives.

In order to understand the Bible in our current context, we must consider other interpretive tools and resources. For instance, John Wesley, the prolific church leader who founded Methodism, suggested that our understanding of God and theology has three additional factors: reason, tradition, and experience. Scripture, reason, tradition, and experience have come to be known as the Wesleyan Quadrilateral.[4]

This aligns with the findings of Rizzuto, who suggests that we *can't* separate from our god concept, which is rooted in our minds (reason), our community (tradition, represented by people of faith who have gone before us and who surround us), and our life story (experience). What we *can* do is be more intentional about all four aspects.

One way to intentionally pursue reason when it comes to your understanding of God is to read books by theologians from different traditions and backgrounds than you. When I began to read theologians who came from different ethnic and cultural backgrounds than I did, I had my mind opened to a whole new way of understanding God and Scripture.

In particular, many theologians that I read had experienced marginalization and suffering in ways I have never encountered as a middle-class white American. Through their writing, I got a glimpse into how those who have been historically oppressed might read the story of the Bible. It was the first time that I realized that most of the Bible was written by people who were experiencing oppression—the Jews in exile and the early Christians under Roman rule. By seeking out the perspective of these scholars, I have come to see God as a liberator in ways my former god concept did not. In turn, my compassion for those who suffer has grown significantly, and I've changed the way I see and live in my city, where many still suffer. As I've learned to think critically, I have been able to use reason when I think about how my faith intersects with politics, current events, and my relationships with those who don't share my worldview or background.

It is equally important to learn from the tradition of communities of faith around you. None of us live alone on an island, even if some of you hard-core introverts daydream about the idea daily. Often when we begin to question our faith, we feel very alone—it is good and healthy to admit this. By looking back at the faith communities that have come before us, and drawing from their experiences, we can soothe that feeling of isolation.

I remember reading about Saint John of the Cross, the Christian mystic I mentioned earlier, who coined the phrase "the dark night of the soul." Reading about his experience led me on a deep journey to discover how many other people in the Christian tradition had faced something similar. When I learned that even Mother Teresa had doubts and wrestled with her faith, I felt so relieved and much less alone. I learned that questions and uncertainty have always been a part of Christian tradition and that God isn't afraid of, and even welcomes, our questions. I now see God as one who is patient with our journey and doesn't expect us to have full understanding in order to take steps of faith one day at a time.

The worldwide experiences of Christians broaden our understanding of tradition. The courage displayed in the underground church in China for the last few decades offers perspective for me as I navigate American society and its various responses to Christianity. My friend Graham Hill leads the Global Church Project,[5] and learning from their stories of Christian traditions all over the world has changed how I understand the story of God and humanity.

Finally, our experiences really matter. We can't change our stories. We can't unwrite what has happened to us or what choices we have made in life. But we can continue to review the *meaning* of our stories. Certain experiences have shaped us deeply, and we've developed a sense of meaning from them. But that sense of meaning doesn't have to be final—in fact, it is possible to find new and different meaning from the same experience. For me, a lot of that work has happened in professional therapy and counseling. I have had a couple different Christian therapists (shout out to those fabulous humans) who have helped me either reshape the meaning of some of my experiences or completely replace one narrative of meaning for another. If the idea of seeing a therapist makes you uneasy, I would love to encourage you to give it a try anyway. These new ways of seeing have set me free.

The next step when it comes to experience is to be intentional about the future experiences you hope will shape your continued growth and formation of your god concept. The unintentional god concept that had been projected on me without my permission created a series of knots I had to untie. It was easy to feel discouraged and like I lacked control. But, somewhere in the messy middle of that process, I stopped seeing myself as a victim of my circumstances and experiences and instead started seeing myself as the one who had my own decisions to make about how I might want to move forward. I put my big-girl pants on and took the wheel of my own discovery process so that I could actively integrate my faith and be intentional about my god concept. There are still days where I don't want to wear my big-girl pants and would rather revert to the lack of agency I once had. Can't someone just give me some easy answers?! I suspect that temptation will always follow me—and I know many people in the later stages of life who can attest to this.

When I finally took responsibility for my experiences, I couldn't worry about disappointing others. Instead of complaining and feeling frustrated about the church I belonged to having little concern for the poor, I expressed gratitude to that community and found a new church. I took the inner angst I felt about not being taught about the mystery of God and directed it toward experiences that helped me press into mystery: spiritual direction, worship services that had traditional liturgical aspects to them, time with Christians who pursue the more charismatic and supernatural experiences with God, and spiritual practices that help me go beyond the limits of intellect to experience God more holistically.

An important part of our experience that I want to highlight is our emotions. When I hear people describe this fourth part of the quadrilateral, it often sounds like emotions are left out of the picture. Rather, I see them as an important aspect of our experience. All of our emotions are real and should be taken into account when we are paying attention to how we have formed our god concept. If we feel a sense of anger or deep fear when we think about God, we should take into account how that is shaping who we are perceiving God to be.

When we validate our emotions and bring them to the other aspects of this quadrilateral, we are more likely to move toward a deeper and hopefully more accurate view of who God is. If we dismiss or disregard our emotions as a factor, we may not give credence to how they are shaping our experience.

The truth is, we do need other people to help us pursue depth in our understanding of God; we just can't rely on their answers to avoid asking our own questions. No single church community of a few hundred people, or one pastor, could be responsible for my discovery about God. The whole church, the church represented by every ethnic group around the world, had a role to play in the growth and depth of my understanding. I learned that I could stay rooted in one small faith community while simultaneously embracing the wholeness that came from exploring how those from West Africa might understand God, or how my Latin American brothers and sisters see Jesus. And at the end of the day, I have the ability to act and step into experiences that take me deeper in the process of picturing God—a process that will be a lifelong journey because we will never arrive at a complete and full understanding of an infinite God.

The Central Mystery

*Once we empty ourselves
of our certainties, we open
ourselves to the mystery.*
—Joan Chittister[1]

Because of my curiosity as a child, fairy tales and mythical characters like Santa Claus didn't last long around my house. I was always looking for the *reasonable* explanation, trying to pry out of my mom how *exactly* Santa got into our apartment since we didn't have a fireplace. Of course, it didn't take long before she caved. My dad didn't last long either after he let it slip that he had seen the tooth fairy leaving me a quarter. I pestered him for a whole evening about what the tooth fairy looked like. Eventually he couldn't keep his story straight and ended up just describing my mom. I figured that one out quickly but begged to still have the tooth fairy visit so I could get the cash.

So you can imagine the challenge my parents faced when they were trying to instill in me faith in a God I couldn't see or touch. Perhaps you have had this experience with your own kids or a niece or nephew. It's so fun to fill their imaginations with the creatures and characters that bring them so much wonder and joy. But there comes a day when kids begin to wonder just what the adults are playing make-believe about and what they are trying to share as a genuine belief. I know some parents who never talk about the Easter Bunny, fairies, or leprechauns for this exact reason. Other parents I know tell me how much joy they find in the imagination of it all! Childhood is full of confusion as kids realize adults are often keeping the whole story from them. Kids are constantly trying to discern which stories are all smoke and mirrors and which stories are rooted in something mysterious but true. They begin their quest to discover their own understanding of truth and fiction.

Bad Analogies, Heresies, and Reductionism

Leaving the mythical characters behind is an early move toward adulthood. After a while, I stopped asking questions about elves and flying reindeer and started asking questions about faith, God, and the spiritual realm. But it was difficult to know which beliefs I should leave behind and which I should cling to. I felt this conflict deeply as a young person, and I have very clear memories of trying to make sense of it all. I remember that the concept of God as Trinity—"three in one"—was one of the earliest concepts that blew my mind when trying to understand God. In many ways it still does!

The first time I can remember hearing about the Trinity was in a blessing we often spoke at my church: in the name of the Father, Son, and Holy Spirit. I soon noticed that in the church I grew up in, we didn't talk too much about the Holy Spirit—it was more like the Father, Son, and holy *Scriptures*! Maybe you have had a similar experience where looking back, one of the persons of the Trinity seems strangely absent. Or perhaps in your experience there was an extreme focus on the Holy Spirit. Even though the word *Trinity* is never used in Scripture, we can see an image of God as "three persons yet one essence" throughout the narrative—from Genesis to Revelation. Even still, one of my personal hang-ups is trying to wrap my head around the concept of God being three and one at the same time. It's so complex!

To combat this complexity, I was given all sorts of analogies and explanations—maybe you've heard some of these, too. For instance, "the Trinity is like water: liquid, ice, and vapor—three forms but one substance." Or "the Trinity is like a tree; it has roots, branches, and fruit, but it's all one tree." Or "the Trinity is like the sun; it's a star with light and heat." The problem, I soon realized, is that every analogy falls short of explaining the mystery of the Trinity. Some analogies have even been called heresy—a belief that falls outside the orthodox teaching of the church.

Throughout Christian history, the punishment for heresy has been severe. Though I don't advocate for this kind of punishment (and I'm glad to say that most branches of the church no longer do either), I do think we ought to reject these simple analogies for the Trinity. All of our human analogies are limited. They all reduce the concept in some way. Or, they all cause reductionism. I appreciate this definition by Randy Peterman:[2]

re·duc·tion·ism \ ri-ˈdŭk-shə-ˌni-zəm \
Theological reductionism is the concept of taking a biblical doctrine and reducing, summarizing, or "boiling the doctrine down" to one finite statement that could very well be an oversimplification.

The temptation for reductionism is why Twitter and theology often don't do well together. When we only have a limited number of characters to work with, we're apt to accidentally— or at times intentionally—produce a reductionistic statement. There are a lot of things that I think pastors and religious leaders overreact about, but I'll join the chorus to warn people against reductionism. If we are going to engage with the mystery of God, then reductionism is the very thing that can keep us from a catechism of curiosity and drop us right back into oversimplified catechisms of certainty.

While this is a pretty harsh criticism of the simplistic answers often found in catechism teaching, the *Catechism of the Catholic Church*, with its 2,865 catechism statements, does have some helpful material. In particular, I can get on board with statement 243 about the Trinity:

> The mystery of the Most Holy Trinity is the central mystery of Christian faith and life. It is the mystery of God in himself. It is therefore the source of all the other mysteries of faith, the light that enlightens them.

Reading this helps me engage the idea that the Trinity is a mystery to be in awe of, not just a theology to be understood. I'll never stop trying to wrap my mind around this concept, even though I am certain I will never be able to fully grasp it. It is the *central* mystery after all. And that means there are other mysteries. In this mind-bending doctrine, I began to find the freedom to step more fully into the mystery of God.

The Family of God

Let me be clear, I'm not rejecting all analogies. Our finite brains need something to grasp onto to help us understand an infinite God. The important thing is to recognize which analogies are helpful and which are reductionistic. If you can move beyond the bad analogies, the Trinity is best thought of as a community or a family. God as parent, Jesus as son, and God's Spirit in a relationship of constant selfless love toward them both. This is unlike any other family we see here on earth (humans seem to have a tough time with the selfless love part). This family isn't a closed family but an invitational family. I often refer to the Trinitarian God as the family of God that is open to us all as we are invited to join in!

The family of God, including us if we want to be a part of it, doesn't exist for itself but rather is a family on mission, a family with the purpose of bringing shalom (or perfect peace), love, and justice to a world that God loves. God leads that effort, but humans are invited to join in every day. If you are willing to be a part of this family, then you are also called to welcome others. Because God's family loves each other well, every member of the family wants each person to participate and to step into their full purpose. The family of God is a "sending" family, not a "holding back" family.

Unfortunately, many of us have been part of a "holding back" family or community. One where we are held back from our potential and purpose. Some families naturally grow and change in ways that allow each member to flourish. That's not always the case; many family systems are difficult and painful. The family of God, at its best, is an empowering family for those who experience support from their earthly family, as well as for those who don't.

Our human relationships can be a helpful analogy in another way—showing us how finite and limited our minds are when it comes to relating to others. I mean, I will be in relationship with my husband for the rest of our lives. But if you've ever met my husband, you know that I'm telling the truth when I say there is no way I am going to be able to completely figure out that strange human! Even if we had 150 years together! We can only take it one day at a time. Some days trying to understand him is exciting, but obviously some days are frustrating. I'm sure he'd agree! I've found this to be true in any type of intimate relationship with roommates, friends, and family. And I've found this to be true in my relationship with God.

We have the ability to not just know *about* God but actually *know* God. At times, trying to understand a divine Being is frustrating—just like relating to other humans. Over the years, I've committed to taking it one step at a time. On the frustrating and hard days when I just don't understand, and in the darkest moments of doubt, I've made a commitment to keep pressing into the questions and to not run from them. Just like I've committed to keep loving my husband and learning about him, even when I feel frustrated and confused by him.

None of this is easy. I've had to choose to love myself enough to keep pushing through when my critical thinking turns into cynicism. I've had to try to love others in my community enough to be patient when they are in a different place in their faith than I am. I've had to make sure that as I try to open my mind to understand God intellectually, I also keep my heart open to experience God relationally, even when I feel confused.

The confusion about God can be overwhelming and disorienting at times. It's like you are in the wilderness with a compass, but the needle is just spinning. The incarnation, or the moment that God put on human form in the person of Jesus, is an opportunity to stop the spinning for at least a moment. Consider the idea that God becoming a human gave us a physical picture of God's character in order to make tangible some of the metaphysical questions. This is how the person of Jesus can be a true north, stopping the needle from spinning long enough for us to regain a sense of direction.

Fullness of Understanding

For years I have been drawn to a beautiful prayer that Paul, an early leader in the first-century church, wrote while in prison because of his faith. He wrote this prayer to a young church he loved in the city of Ephesus, and you can read it in the Bible in Ephesians 3:14–21. Notice the way that Paul weaves through the persons of the Trinity in his prayer:

> For this reason I kneel before the Father, from whom every family in heaven and on earth derives its name. I pray that out of his glorious riches he may strengthen you with power through his Spirit in your inner being, so that Christ may dwell in your hearts through faith. And I pray that you, being rooted and established in love, may have power, together with all the Lord's holy people, to grasp how wide and long and high and deep is the love of Christ, and to know this love that surpasses knowledge—that you may be filled to the measure of all the fullness of God.

> Now to him who is able to do immeasurably more
> than all we ask or imagine, according to his power that
> is at work within us, to him be glory in the church and
> in Christ Jesus throughout all generations, for ever and
> ever! Amen.[3]

In so many ways, I wish that the "measure of the fullness of God" that Paul is talking about would be the fullness of *understanding* God. But clearly Paul's prayer is for people like me, and probably you, who endlessly seek knowledge; he prays that we will be filled by God's *relational* love—the love that *surpasses* knowledge. When our finite minds hit their inevitable limitations, we need the love that can go further than our understanding. The fullness that Paul refers to here is about experience, not knowledge. His prayer is that the experience of God's love will be full in the midst of our limited ability to understand.

When I pray, I tend to offer prayers that sound more like, "God, I have imagined how I'd like this to turn out, so if you could work it out, right in the timing I'm hoping for and in a way that doesn't stress me out, that would be great." Which couldn't be more different from Paul's prayer here that God will do even *more* than we could imagine. Not just a little more, but so much more that we wouldn't even be able to measure it. I'm better able to pray this way, along with Paul, on some days more than others.

Even today, when I stop to think about it, it is still so mysterious how this family of God with its Trinitarian leadership really works and at times still feels frustrating! The fact that God cannot be fully comprehended can move from being mostly frustrating to also being exciting.

Although I often long for clarity, certainty, and simplicity when it comes to understanding God, the reality is that I don't think I would really be able to believe in, or have faith in, a god that my human mind could understand. I mean, how small would that god be? Would a god I can fully comprehend be worthy of worship? I can get excited about the idea that my relationship with God, rather than just knowledge about God, means that I am always learning more in a constant pursuit of intimacy with a complex yet relational God.

When Faith Is What You Fear

The opposite of faith is not doubt, but certainty. Certainty is missing the point entirely. Faith includes noticing the mess, the emptiness and discomfort, and letting it be there until some light returns.
—Anne Lamott

My friend James remembers the day that he began to reckon with the concept of uncertainty. James is a gastroenterologist—a medical doctor who specializes in treating conditions affecting digestion and nutrition. Think of your esophagus, stomach, intestines, liver, and pancreas. In effect, it means he deals with some gross (to me!) and amazing (to him!) stuff every day. Given his specific areas of expertise, he is a man of many stories—some funny, some tragic, some triumphant, some humbling. I've known him for a while, but when he speaks of how he came to be who he is as a physician—the failures, the questioning of purpose, and the discovery of meaning in the profound relationships he gets to build with people who are hurting—I understand him, and myself, better.

When James was in his third year of medical school and beginning his clinical work, he wrestled with the reality that when he left the classroom, the things that once seemed very black and white on a test or in a paper were now much more nuanced. Now that he was seeing actual patients, there was so much more uncertainty. It made him feel, perhaps for the first time in his life, like he was stupid. In a moment of overwhelming discouragement, he confessed how he felt to an attending, a senior physician. He asked this attending, "Is it normal to feel stupid? Because I feel stupid all the time."

The doctor paused for a moment before answering, and in the ensuing silence James thought for a moment he had really blown it by being so honest. "I've just ruined my career before it's started!" the voice in his head bemoaned.

In the midst of his wallowing, he noticed a sense of profound empathy in the attending's eyes, and the doctor said something that James would never forget. "If you ever stop

feeling stupid, you are at a moment in your career
are going to truly hurt a patient."

With tears in his eyes, the doctor went on to share about
how each time he got "too big for his britches," there was a
complicated case or a difficult outcome that brought him back
to earth. Having to share with a patient or their family that
something didn't go according to plan was humbling. Those
experiences reminded him that feeling stupid, and being honest about where he was at, was better than thinking he had it
all figured out. James said that was the day that he realized that
uncertainty was always going to be a part of his work as well as
all other aspects of his life.

As a physician, James actually risks danger to others if he
tries to force certainty. Similarly, in our lives of faith, our obsession with certainty can lead us to dangerous spaces. And the
most dangerous space is one that says faith equals certainty. In
reality, certainty and faith cannot coexist. To be certain is to
know for sure, making faith unnecessary. Writer Anne Lamott
is often quoted explaining, "The opposite of faith is not doubt,
but certainty." I define faith as putting your trust and hope in
something in spite of the fact that you can't be certain. It's a
willingness to commit without knowing all you'd like to know.
And that means risk.

There is always more to know and to learn, but at some
point we reach the edge of our knowledge or ability to understand. It's there on that cliff you have to choose if you will
jump into uncertainty or try to convince yourself of the myth

of certainty. This is the decision that James faces every day. Despite all the uncertainty that exists in medicine, James strives to partner with his patient as they commit to a plan of treatment, a course through the unknown. In his words, "I share the burden of uncertainty with them, so that neither of us feel alone." Every day is a new challenge full of new questions. So it is in the life of faith.

Attitude Adjustment

When I was in college, there was a professor named Daniel Taylor, and he had written a book called *The Myth of Certainty*. He was beloved by his students and had the reputation for being the kind of mentor who would listen to you and help you process your questions about life, relationships, and faith. He always resisted giving easy answers. Most people would leave his office with more questions than they came in with. But it was precisely the excitement and intrigue of having their minds opened to deeper questions that drew students to him. He cultivated the curiosity within these budding young adults. Sometimes it was difficult and frustrating, but it helped them feel more alive. And that is a feeling everyone is drawn to.

The line from Professor Taylor's book that has stuck with me is this, "The demand for certainty inevitably creates its opposite—doubt. Doubt derives its strength from those who fear it most."[1] Taylor suggests that our attitude toward doubt and uncertainty is more important than eliminating doubt.

This was a profound realization for me in college. I always felt that doubt was something to be feared, combated, squelched, or avoided at all costs. Doubt meant you weren't a good Christian—or worse, weren't a Christian at all! Much of this is rooted in bad exegesis of some classic doubt passages in Scripture (which we will talk more about in part 2). But Taylor suggests the opposite! That doubt is a natural, normal part of a life of faith, and complete certainty is a myth.

Taylor shows us that doubt shouldn't be something we try to crush or demolish, because it can be made to *serve* our faith. Instead of seeing doubt as something "sapping faith's strength," the very presence of doubt gives faith its reason for being. Taylor says, "Clearly faith is not needed where certainty supposedly exists, but only in situations where doubt is possible, even present."[2]

What Are We Afraid Of?

I think faith is something that we fear, because faith means accepting the role of doubt and uncertainty. It means that we can no longer pretend that certainty is real and attainable. We have to admit that we are finite humans pursuing an infinite God. We have limitations. Every day we have the choice to commit and to step out in faith or not. This happens in big ways (like choosing to believe in God at all) and small ways (like trusting the sense you have that God is leading you to make a particular decision). We are afraid to act based on faith because those steps of faith never come with certainty. But if we choose faith, we must accept the reality of uncertainty.

Greg Boyd, a pastor in my city, wrote a book called *The Benefit of the Doubt*. He uses the phrase "certainty-seeking faith" to describe people whose main objective in their life of faith is to pursue certainty. Of course we should pursue truth, but the idea that we can reach complete certainty has devastating consequences for Christians and people who are trying to follow and trust Jesus. First of all, it lacks any sense of humility or an acknowledgment that we could be wrong. It keeps us from continuing to wonder. Finally, it keeps us from engaging with people who are different from us and who may have a different perspective. Most importantly, Boyd suggests that "certainty-seeking faith" has led many to "mistakenly interpret the doctrine that we're 'saved by faith' to mean we're 'saved by feeling certain about particular beliefs.'"[2] This is dangerous because it means certainty becomes the object of worship rather than God.

For instance, someone could agree intellectually with the statement: "Jesus is Savior and Lord." But intellectual assent is not equivalent to faith. Faith comes with all kinds of questions: If Jesus is Savior, what is he saving you from? What is he saving you for? If he is Lord, that means he is a leader. If Jesus is your leader, how is he leading you currently? What direction are you going with Jesus as your leader rather than someone else, or rather than only trusting your own leadership? It is possible to believe that a statement is certain and true without it having any practical impact on how you live your life. But true *faith* will always deeply impact our lives.

The early Christians viewed the world quite differently than we do in our modern context. The definition of belief as an "intellectual agreement" with some sort of fact or proposition would be lost on them. They saw the mind, body, and spirit as working holistically. Beliefs impacted a person's way of life, not just their way of thinking.

When faith becomes merely intellectual agreement, it becomes separated from our way of life. One way I see this dichotomy manifesting itself in the world is the rise of Moralistic Therapeutic Deism (MTD). MTD is perhaps the most dominant worldview held by millennials and generation Z, according to some recent research.[3] MTD consists of five core beliefs: (1) A god exists who created and ordered the world and who watches over human life on earth. (2) God wants people to be good, nice, and fair to each other, as taught in the Bible and by most world religions. (3) The central goal of life is to be happy and to feel good about oneself. (4) God does not need to be particularly involved in one's life except when God is needed to resolve a problem. (5) Good people go to heaven when they die.[4]

Upon first glance, this worldview sounds appealing, but my experience coming alongside others is that the MTD paradigm isn't a very sturdy base for facing life's challenges. I think that younger people are embracing MTD because it allows you to avoid the work that comes with overcoming the fears associated with faith. It's easier to have a loose sense of the Divine and call on God when you are "in need" than to choose to wonder, discover, and be curious about God. This way of thinking leads to an experience of a god that is more like a cosmic vending machine than a relationship—push B3 for a peace that passes understanding, or C5 for a really hot spouse, or A2 for kids who don't struggle in school. A relationship like that with another human would never fly. So is it realistic to relate to God this way? Apparently, many people in America think so, enough that some sociologists are calling MTD "the new American religion." I see MTD as an unfortunate barrier that keeps someone from truly staying curious.

Faith Is a Verb

So back to my definition of faith: "putting your trust and hope in something in spite of the fact that you can't be certain." For the writers of the Bible, for those who lived at the time of Jesus, for the early church, and for Jesus himself, *faith* was a verb, not a noun. We typically see both *faith* and *hope* as nouns. But if faith and belief, as we read about them in the Bible, are active, then they really are actions of trusting and hoping. Faith in Jesus means *trusting* Jesus by taking actions that might be risky when God leads you. Faith in God means actively *hoping* that life will offer peace, or shalom—a peace that passes all understanding—even when our reason, logic, and certainty hit their limits. When Jesus speaks with Nicodemus at night in

John 3, the word *believe* is used seven times in just a few verses. Every time, including the infamous John 3:16, it is used as a verb in the Greek, not a noun.[5]

Faith is a verb because it causes you to live differently, even when you are unsure! It's not that you have figured out the right set of beliefs in order to be "saved"; nor are those who have not figured it out "damned." If we think faith means getting it right and being certain, it's no wonder faith terrifies us! It's impossible to be fully certain. This fear of faith can be paralyzing. It can leave us deserted in the wilderness, frozen at the base of the wall (something I want us to unpack in the next chapter). In an honest moment, we know if we start to press into this deeper understanding of faith, it will mean accepting uncertainty, and that can be scary.

So we have a choice to make. Just like James as a physician needed to decide if he could continue to practice medicine when total certainty wasn't an option, we have to decide if we will keep exploring our faith even though we can't reach complete certainty. Sometimes we find ourselves immobilized by fear, but we don't have to stay there. Part 2 of this book will explore the various wilderness experiences we face in life and offer steps to get unstuck. I agree with Taylor that certainty is a myth. But "commitment to faith is a risk worth taking."[6] It's the reason I'm pouring out my heart to you in this book. Just because I think it's worth it doesn't mean risk is easy. But everything worth doing comes with some degree of challenge.

People often ask me, "Are you afraid of people in your church doubting their faith or questioning God or the Bible?" My honest reply is that I am more afraid that they won't.

I'm afraid that those I lead won't stay curious.

I'm convinced that stepping toward questions and doubts rather than running from them leads to a life of curiosity. And people who stay curious are more likely to live a holistic, verb-based faith, one that is life changing—vibrant and full of reflection, wonder, and complexity. When people are stuck, paralyzed by fear, their faith appears dull and lacks connection to the rest of their life. I'd rather people take the risk—knowing that they might end up walking away from faith for a while or altogether—because what I see on the other side has such great potential for their well-being.

I'd rather lead the question askers and the stone turners than the apathetic and unengaged. I get excited to be in community with the wrestlers and the explorers, not the certainty seekers and truth defenders. Martin Luther King Jr. said that "courage is an inner resolution to go forward despite obstacles."[7] Notice he didn't say that courage is the absence of fear. In fact, fear is a common obstacle. And it's not the only one.

Even though you might be afraid of what may be under the stones you will overturn or what may lie at the other end of the wilderness, courage means making an "inner resolution" to start taking steps anyway.

Hitting the Wall

*God gave you brains, so don't go
drown in your own thinkings. God gave
you hands so you could pick up your
broken pieces, God gave you feet so
you can find your own way home.*
—*"The Great Unknown," Cloud Cult*

We all have doubts and questions, and none of our stories are exactly the same. Nevertheless, some overlapping themes have emerged in my countless conversations with those who are wrestling with doubt. Many people describe a season of questions and doubts as a wilderness experience. Others describe the experience of "hitting the wall." In the book *The Critical Journey*, Janet Hagberg and Robert Guelich describe the various stages of faith, including one common stage: "the wall."

The Wall

- A profound time of seeking understanding, trying to reconcile various life experiences with one's faith.
- A season where we must face our brokenness, the brokenness of others, and the brokenness of our communities.
- A time when we can no longer hide from the questions and doubts, and we begin to confront what is really going on deep inside of us.

To hit the wall, then, signifies an incredibly difficult part in our journey of faith and meaning. It is so uncomfortable, in fact, and takes so much courage to go through it that many people avoid hitting the wall in the first place! When they see something tall and scary-looking in the distance, they do whatever they can, internally and externally, to avoid it. So if you are willing to wonder your way through the journey until you reach the wall, you are already courageous! I often say it is totally *normal* to hit the wall, but it's not *typical*. Most people avoid the wall altogether or refuse to acknowledge it. When people hit the wall, some feel concerned that they are "crazy," "strange," or "weird." Not at all! This is totally normal, but few people have the courage to face the wall head on.

If you have not yet hit the wall yourself, you have probably seen others close to you smack right into it. Perhaps you have been through this spiritually in the past. Maybe you are in the midst of it now. Possibly you can see it coming on the horizon. The most important thing to realize is this: *encountering a wall is a sign that your spiritual life is growing and maturing.*

Unfortunately, the church has often communicated the opposite. Those who are open in expressing their doubts and fears are often the ones that concern church leaders the most, while those who seem to never waver are celebrated as mature Christians with the deepest faith. In reality, those who are willing to face the wall and begin the intentional process of going through it are the ones who will come out on the other side with the most profound and vibrant faith.

From Knowing to Seeking

My first experience of hitting the wall was less than ideal, although frankly there's never a good time to take a face-plant into a stack of bricks. I was in my first job after graduating college, and I had been entrusted to lead 150 freshmen on a college campus. My job was to live in the residence hall with these students; I was responsible for overseeing the space in which they would grow spiritually, emotionally, and intellectually.

(Why they let a twenty-two-year-old supervise a giant group of eighteen-year-olds I will never understand!)

Some days, it was all I could do to keep them alive. I could tell you stories for hours about the levels of absurdity college freshmen will go to in order to rationalize their decisions to destroy property or set something on fire. I could share the horrors of overflowing urinals, broken bones, and the drama of the triangulation that happens when three freshmen women live in a tiny dorm room designed for two. I won't tell you those stories, because it will only make you more convinced that I had no business in that role in the first place.

I had seen the wall on the horizon for a year or two before slamming into it as I stepped into my role as a leader—no longer a *student* leader, an actual leader. Because of my new role and corresponding responsibilities, I found it an awkward time to be wrestling with so many doubts, fears, and uncertainties. I had no good answers. I couldn't even pray for those I led, and I often couldn't clear my own mind in order to offer anything helpful.

What I learned during that time is that avoiding the wall doesn't work. Trying to go around, under, or over or even trying to ignore the wall makes this season of life worse.

We have to go through it.

Going through the wall is not something we do only once. Since then, I have had other wall experiences in my life. When you are willing to face a wall in your life, you will inevitably face multiple. Each time, I've had to do the hard work of going through, brick by brick, and I've never regretted it.

Those who are willing to move through the wall start by seeking direction rather than answers. Hagberg and Guelich say that moving through the wall means moving from "a posture of knowing to one of seeking."[1] Think about how different those two postures are from each other. If we take on a posture of seeking, we begin to break through the wall brick by brick with the patience it takes to try to discover what each brick means. Why was that brick there? What do I do with it now that it's not a part of this wall anymore? Seeking is what gives us curiosity, which leads to the endurance to keep going even when it's hard or tiring. Even when it can seem scary and discouraging.

What We Do When We Hit the Wall

People respond to hitting the wall in a variety of ways. Here are a few—and I've experienced them all!

The Wall Avoiders

Some people avoid the wall altogether, avoiding feeling the blow of hitting the wall. This is the most common response, and my observation is that many of these people go on to have a relationship with God that works for them. However, given that they have never done the hard work that comes with going through the wall, they haven't built the same capacity and strength needed to face the more difficult realities in life. For instance, it's harder for them to stay in conversations with people who disagree with them. Since they have often tried to avoid the pain of hitting the wall, it's difficult to engage in the suffering of others.

At times, this avoidance can also result in a faith that feels dull and rote. In order to keep from hitting the wall, this person will often simply go through the motions in a sort of mechanical way. They find quick justifications for things they don't understand, rather than pressing into the questions. They often try to change the subject when there is disagreement in a conversation, labeling it too political or divisive. They say or think things like, "Can we talk about something more lighthearted and stop focusing on the negative?" or "Whenever I feel confused, I need to remember to have faith like a child and just trust God more."

The song these wall avoiders have on repeat: "Happy" by Pharrell Williams.

The Wall Ignorers

Another way to avoid the wall is to see it coming and turn the other way—returning to a stage of wandering in order to "find yourself." Wall ignorers don't avoid the wall altogether but try to ignore it. Ignoring the wall shows up in all sorts of behaviors, from spending money you don't have, to avoiding responsibility at work, to avoiding commitment in relationships. If these folks are participating in a church or faith community, it is often sporadic and noncommittal as well. Some are church "roamers," who determine where they want to venture for a worship service by how they are feeling that morning. Or maybe they decide they feel like brunch instead. (To be honest, I totally get that—I love brunch.) These folks often say things like, "I'll deal with these questions in the future, when I settle down and get married . . . when I get a job in the field I want to be in . . . when I have kids . . . when I hit my thirties . . . no my forties." Constant excuses help them push off the reality of what they are facing. But in the end, waiting for the next milestone becomes the millstone around their neck, holding them back from the growth they could be experiencing right now.

The song wall ignorers have on repeat: "Wake Me Up" by Avicii.

The Wall Pouters

Others run into the wall and are so discouraged by the experience that they sit down at the base of the wall, cross their arms, and sulk. While this can be a perfectly acceptable initial response, staying in a pouting position is not recommended. Those who stay immersed in this place are often confused why others aren't hitting the wall. Misery loves company, and wall pouters often complain: "Why aren't others asking these questions? They must not be willing to be honest with their doubts. Why aren't my friends outraged by the hypocrisy of some Christians? How can they still go to *that* church with *that* pastor who said *that* thing on Facebook? No one around me understands what it's like to actually be in pain because I know they haven't suffered like I have." Those who sit down at the foot of the wall and refuse to get up typically end up dealing with bitterness and fewer close relationships. Sometimes their focus on their own pain keeps them from examining their own privilege and its effect on others.

The song the wall pouters have on repeat: "Interlude: Moving On" by Paramore.

The Wall Doubters

I have to give props to this final group of people, who get at least an E for effort! These are the folks who hit the wall, shake off the blow, and look at the wall with a sense of optimism. They figure, "There has *got* to be a way over this thing . . . or maybe around it? Perhaps we could find a shovel and dig under it?" They realize that going through the wall is not going to be easy, so they brainstorm to think of *any other way* to overcome their predicament—leading to many failed attempts. They seriously doubt that they'll need to go through this thing brick by brick and try to find an easier method when it comes to working through their questions.

Perhaps they find a new guru with a spirituality blog or podcast. All of a sudden, everything this new person says is gold, and the wall doubter begins to put all their eggs in this guru's proverbial basket. Others think they've overcome their wall by excluding certain people or experiences from their lives.

Some simply stop going to church and participating in organized religion and claim, sometimes very publicly, that they're better off. Or they just avoid that side of their family with whom they disagree about what it means to be a Jesus follower. These actions remind me of the cliché "throwing the baby out with the bathwater." People discard something that seems easy to let go of at the time but that will have to be dealt with at some point.

Or these eager ones will start yoga, meditation, or some of the Ignatian practices I mentioned earlier—all good things! But I am concerned when it sounds like they're using them as a silver bullet to avoid some of the deeper questions the wall raises. I also get worried that avoiding community causes someone to feel a false sense of relief because they aren't choosing a discipline of being in relationship with people who they are different from and may disagree with. It's easy to pour ourselves into personal betterment, vocational goals and development, and career or family benchmarks in order to convince ourselves this wall can be scaled! I love strategic planning, but no amount of "Power Sheets" or "Your Best Year Yet" journals will get you out of the brick-by-brick work of going through the spiritual wall.

The song the wall doubters have on repeat: "Higher Love" by Steve Winwood.

The Wall Breakers

It is possible to go through the wall brick by brick, and the result of doing that work almost always pays off spiritually and emotionally. Wall breakers are people who are willing to do the work to break through. But you can't say *break through* without *break*. Something will always get broken—a broken heart, broken relationships, shattered dreams that were not based in reality. The brokenness in our lives comes in many forms. Yet, the wall needs to be broken down brick by brick, and in our brokenness we can choose to persevere.

The apostle Paul was trying to encourage the young church in Rome, and as paraphrased by Eugene Peterson, he said, "We continue to shout our praise even when we're hemmed in with troubles, because we know how troubles can develop passionate patience in us, and how that patience in turn forges the tempered steel of virtue, keeping us alert for whatever God will do next. In alert expectancy such as this, we're never left feeling shortchanged."[2]

I don't think Paul knew anything about brain chemistry in the first century, but I love how modern science confirms the encouragement he wrote in this letter. Studies have shown that those who go through suffering and difficulties grow in their ability to persevere. Psychologists are now calling this increase of emotional and mental strength Post Traumatic Growth.[3] This is not to minimize Post Traumatic Stress Disorder (PTSD), because that is very real and damaging. However, when those who've been through trauma and suffering come through the difficult intentional process of breaking through the wall, there is a promise of growth on the other side. This is true even for those who choose to get help when they suffer from PTSD. The signs of Post Traumatic Growth are appreciation for life, relationships with others, new possibilities in life, personal strength, and spiritual change.[4] That last factor is most likely to happen when the wall we are facing is connected to wrestling with our faith.

Wall breakers say or think things like, "I just need to take this one day at a time; I don't have to figure everything out all at once" or "Is there someone I need to invite to support me intentionally in this season?" or "How might I pursue additional spaces for growth so my faith community is not solely responsible for my formation?" or "I wonder what I can try next since I'm feeling stuck where I'm at."

Often the very things that led us to hit the wall reveal to us the first bricks we need to begin to chip away at—beginning a process that leads to freedom. To engage these realities, we have to make the choice to stay curious, to choose to engage with all that comes, and to go through the wall brick by brick. Breakthrough is possible, but it means we risk acknowledging our brokenness along the way.

There are many songs I can imagine those who choose to stay curious and become wall breakers will have on repeat. My current favorite: "The Great Unknown" by Cloud Cult.

God gave you brains, so don't go drown in your own thinkings. God gave you hands so you could pick up your broken pieces. God gave you feet so you can find your own way home.

PART 2

Overcoming the
Obstacles

Expansion Plan

*It's the very nature of wonder to catch
us off guard, to circumvent expectations
and assumptions. Wonder can't be
packaged, and it can't be worked up.
It requires some sense of being there
and some sense of engagement.*
—Eugene H. Peterson

I live in Minnesota where we joke that there are only two seasons: winter and road construction.

If you mention this joke to someone, it will receive a hearty groan because we've all heard it a thousand times. Every moment without snow, ice, and frigid temperatures is full of road construction. Obviously, there are only so many months where the climate makes it reasonable to get this type of outside work done. But road construction is so prevalent in Minnesota because the ice and the snow cause so much damage to the roads themselves. The snow falls, melts, freezes, melts, freezes, more snow falls, it melts, freezes, and so on. Every time the snow melts, it seeps into the cracks, large or small, in the road.

When water freezes it expands by about 9 percent, and this expansion has enough force to break concrete and asphalt. This creates potholes and cracks in the road that have been known to cause hubcaps to go flying. Water is actually unique. Most liquids *contract* when they freeze because the molecules are more tightly packed. The way that hydrogen bonds with oxygen creates the opposite effect, and thus water expands slowly in the freezing process.

Humans are like water. I don't mean literally, although Bill Nye the Science Guy would be quick to remind us that the average adult male is 60 percent water. What I mean is that some seasons in our lives cause us to expand. It can happen slowly over time. Sometimes we don't notice it happening. What we *do* notice is the potholes and cracks in our lives where a nice clear path used to be. We begin to experience a bumpy ride because our expansion has literally broken through what seemed so solid.

You can see how easily this expansion can be mistaken for something negative. But what you are experiencing is a form of growth. We tend to think of growth as linear, moving forward on a scale or higher up on the ladder of achievement. While this may be true when it comes to growth in education or business, when it comes to spiritual growth, we expand.

The Narrow Place

In the narrative of Scripture, the wilderness is an expansion space. In one of the first wilderness stories in Scripture, Moses leads the Hebrew people out of Egypt. The Hebrews used the word *Mizraim* as the common name for Egypt, which means "the narrow place." God was leading them out of the narrow place. While they were enslaved by the Egyptians, the Hebrews grew in number; they expanded. The narrow place was too tight for them to continue to survive.

Pharaoh had a different plan to deal with the expansion of the Hebrew people: kill the baby boys. He figured that would help curb the population growth. If the Hebrews expand too much, they would become a threat.

God's response to the expansion of the Hebrew people was to help them *pass through* the Red Sea by parting the waters. This led them into the wilderness, with the goal of reaching the promised land on the other side. They would encounter more drama and trauma on the way to that land, but Exodus adamantly reinforces that God was with them *every* moment they were in the wilderness. Even so, the people doubted God constantly. They even asked if they could return to Egypt, to the narrow place. That's how frustrating the wilderness can be—it causes you to want to shove your expanded self back into something that doesn't fit anymore. Like the coat your parents tried to squeeze you into to save money even after you'd outgrown it.

When they arrived at the promised land, it was time to live up to their name once again. This time the water from the Jordan River stopped flowing from upstream, and the Hebrews were able to walk through the river bed to the other side and begin the next stage in their life with God.

The exodus narrative lays out the following pattern for us: expansion in the narrow place, passing through into the wilderness, doubting God in the wilderness, asking God if you can go back to the narrow place, finally passing through to the next destination, and realizing that new destination isn't a finish line but the start of a new chapter.

We are not likely to experience a journey like this literally, but most of us will experience it spiritually. We find ourselves in narrow places all the time. It might be a relationship, a job, or a faith community. As we begin to expand, we feel the strain until the expansion cracks the asphalt like ice in a pothole or busts the seams like the jacket that was too tight. When we find ourselves in narrow places, it's likely we will have to pass through. You don't always have a clear direction, but you can't stay here. And as you pass through you find yourself in the wilderness.

Scary versus Dangerous

The rest of this book is about how to move through the wilderness, or break through the wall, whichever metaphor feels like it fits. You have expanded as a person; you are asking questions you never thought you would ask. The pavement that once seemed solid is cracked and broken. When you look back at the path behind you, the Red Sea has closed again so that you can't go back. In the rest of these pages, we are going to name some of the obstacles that prevent us from moving from wandering to wondering, confusion to reflection, skepticism to action, certainty to conviction.

One of my hobbies is to read stories and listen to podcasts about entrepreneurs. I'm fascinated by stories of beginnings. In nearly every story of someone starting something awesome, they describe a moment where they came to a crossroads. Jim Koch, the cofounder of Boston Beer Company, producers of Samuel Adams beer, says, "There are things in life that are scary, but not dangerous, but we're scared of them. And then there are things that are dangerous, but not scary. And those are the real problem. Those are the issue."[1] Koch came to a crossroads in his life where he knew that if moved forward, it would be *scary* because he would be stepping deeper into uncertainty. But if he held back it would be *dangerous* because it would be the beginning of the end of a dream. If he hadn't moved forward, even though he was scared, he never would have built a company that has become so successful.

If you are expanding spiritually, there is a whole wilderness of uncertainty ahead of you. It's no doubt scary to stay curious because asking questions is risky when we don't know where the answers will lead us. Or we might wonder if we will be able to find any answers at all! Even though moving into the great unknown is scary (we will talk about confronting fear in chapter 13), staying where you are is dangerous. Just like it was dangerous for the Hebrews to stay in Egypt. Moving forward doesn't mean that there is nothing to fear, but staying where you are will be the beginning of the end of a faith you can actually live with. It's not a good expansion plan to stay where you are at. You need to pass through.

Experimenting: Moving in Order to Gain Perspective

Imagine that you are in a beautiful place with small hills and valleys. Your friend suggested this particular location because there is a beautiful spring-fed pond surrounded by willow trees and amazing wildlife. Hoping to find the perfect place to relax, you are disappointed to arrive and see no pond, no willow trees, and no wildlife as far as your eyes can see.

"Oh well," you think to yourself, "my friend must have been mistaken. I see hills and valleys and some huge pine trees, but no pond." Hanging your head in disappointment, you go back to the car wondering if you can make it home in time to binge the new season of your favorite show on Netflix before you have to be ready for work in the morning.

If you trusted your friend, you would have assumed that the pond was there and that you had to search a bit in order to discover it. You may have to walk through the forest of pines or climb a few of those hills in order to find the willow trees and wildlife your friend described. Just because you don't see it from the parking lot doesn't mean it's not there. When we move, our vantage point changes. As we put one foot in front of the other, we see things that we couldn't see before.

Sure enough, even though you are a bit sweaty and tired from the hike, you come around a bend and there it is! Beautiful, just as your friend has described it. The stream flowing into the pond is magical, with reeds swaying in its banks. Sitting down to rest under the tree feels even better because of the work you put in to arrive there.

René Descartes famously said, "I think, therefore I am." Not to disagree with a seventeenth-century philosopher, but I want to take it a bit further. I would like to say, "I move, therefore I am."

Movement is a sign of life. It means we are still breathing, still alive, still able to see new perspectives and vantage points.

When we feel stuck, it may mean we need some time to rest, think, or pray, but first, we must remember to move! Through moving, we collect experiences we can then process at the edge of the pond. Moving opens us up to other possibilities we could not see before. We may get curious, wonder where that little creek leads, and decide to follow it upstream. We may imagine other potentials that cause us to question if there could be more. Maybe this stream runs into a larger body of water or becomes a waterfall!

So what do we do when faced with this type of intersection in our lives? How do we pass through in the midst of uncertainty?

We need to move in order to pass through the wilderness or wall. Taking actions that help our minds and hearts open up can bring new perspectives on what direction we need to take. The best way to begin to take action to expand your perspective is through what I like to call *experiments*.

Now, I'm not talking about the kind of experiments you did in high-school chemistry. However, let's borrow some of the scientific process here. Any good experiment has a few components that are crucial.

First, you have a question you want to answer.

Second, you design a process you think could help you answer the question.

Third, you follow those steps intentionally.

Finally, you review your results to see what you have learned.

This is exactly what I am proposing you do when it comes to God, spirituality, and the questions you're facing. The first step would be to identify the question you're asking. Here are some that I hear often from people I've talked with:

- Why does God allow so much suffering in the world?
- How can there be so much division among one human-ity that God created?
- Does the church really have any relevance to my life after having been disconnected for years?
- Will I ever be able to experience God again in my life after feeling so distant?
- Can I reconcile my understanding of faith with the reality of science?

Let's use that last question as an example. It's the kind that typically opens up even deeper questions. I find this to be the reason some people avoid moving into their questions. They don't want to pull on the thread, knowing it will lead to more and more difficult questions they feel ill equipped to answer. I urge you to consider how more questions, although daunting, can actually be a really good, and exciting, part of life.

So, let's think about what types of experiments you could try in order to move further down the path toward discovery.

You could find a book or two on the subject of science and faith—or even get a couple other people to read together and discuss for the sake of greater discovery. You could find someone in your wider network you think is a brilliant scientist who is also a Christian and see how they answer this question. You could also do this with an atheist or someone with another worldview. It wouldn't be too difficult to spend some time watching a documentary or experiencing nature—opening yourself up spiritually in order to see if God impresses something upon your mind or heart.

As you can see, it isn't difficult to come up with a list of ways to explore the question. Unfortunately, I find people typically stop before taking any action. They may come up with a question, and in some cases, even a list of potential action steps, but they never start the actual experiment. If they do begin the experiment, there are usually a few other roadblocks to discovery.

If your process is haphazard and not very clear from the beginning, you're going to run into problems. Experiments that are unorganized or poorly conducted don't lend themselves to a reliable data set. Ask any chemistry teacher. If your process is sloppy, more than likely your results will be as well. This leads to a distrust of your results—in this case, your learnings.

Another reality that holds us back from discovery is that we often skip the final step: reviewing your results to see what you have learned.

The process of review needs to be intentional and communal. In chemistry, reports are written on the results of the experiment so that the greater scientific community can learn from the experiment and its findings can be passed on for others to build upon. Others will try to replicate the experiment to confirm the findings or adjust it to learn more. Similarly, the scientific and academic communities do not take a report seriously if it's not peer reviewed. A peer-reviewed report provides the deepest learning, for its results have been discovered not only by experimenter(s) but also by others trusted within the community.

Studies have shown that the only way that people truly make it through the wall is with the help of "process-oriented relationships." This can be with a pastor or mentor, a therapist or counselor, a small group from your church or community, or a sibling, spouse, friend, or prayer partner. These kinds of relationships can happen in a variety of ways, but to get through the wall, they must happen.

Process-oriented relationships are more than just friends hanging out or swapping stories about the woes of raising toddlers or the stress of grad school. While it's great to have those relationships, process-oriented relationships are more intentional. It may mean having an awkward conversation with a friend in which you express that you're hoping you can both engage in an intentional process of discovery together. Or it may mean giving some sort of group a try even though you are hesitant. But it's worth it. You need to be able to answer this question: Who are your people for this journey?

To explore some of life's deepest questions you will need to try many experiments to find direction. However, nearly all experiments, if following a process, will move you. They will help you get unstuck. Rarely do one or two experiments end with a big reveal, but even the small things learned along the way matter and take us deeper. Experiments take effort, but the wonder they can open up in our lives about who Jesus is, who we are, and why we exist can change everything.

Here are examples of some ways you can approach your experiments based on the example questions I gave above.

Why Does God Allow So Much Suffering in the World?

You could:

- Engage in relationship with someone who is suffering and intentionally listen to them and ask good questions.
- Spend time with a group of people who have experienced oppression or significant injustice. In many cities, it's not hard to get connected to refugees, many of whom have had difficult journeys.
- Spend time in a care center with people experiencing long-term illness.
- Don't probe, but let people share their difficult experiences with you and listen for how they respond to these experiences.

These experiments will not give you a pat answer to your question (you're not looking for pat answers anyway), but they can take you to a whole new world of understanding.

How Can There Be So Much Division among One Humanity That God Created?

You could:

- Interview two people on opposite sides of a debate or political spectrum.
- Deepen a relationship with someone who is very different from you, maybe even someone with whom you deeply disagree on an issue.
- Read books from various perspectives on an issue with the goal of understanding—not merely agreeing.
- Take a deeper look at the history of countries like the United States and try to understand the roots of the hostility that still exists today between groups of people.

Does the Church Really Have Any Relevance to My Life after Having Been Disconnected for Years?

You could:

- Ask people who have left the church why they stayed away.
- Interview people who chose to go back to church after time away from organized religion.
- Try different expressions of Christianity than the one you are used to.
- Give yourself a due date for the review and try going to the same church every week for three months. Perhaps reentering as a fully formed adult will open up new perspectives and understanding from what you experienced in adolescence.

Will I Ever Be Able to Experience God Again in My Life after Feeling So Distant?

You could try a series of experiments where you test out new spiritual practices.

- Never journaled? Commit to journaling every day for a month.
- Never tried connecting to God through movement? Take some classes and wonder as you participate—can I experience God through this dance, yoga, swimming?
- Never been one to take nature walks? See if you notice anything spiritually after a few weeks of intentional listening to creation around you.

I have no idea what direction you will be going by the end of these experiments. But I do know that you would not be sitting still, wandering, or stuck. You'll be moving in a new direction, and that is a great place to start.

Each chapter in this section will offer experiment ideas in response to the obstacles that are named. You may be intrigued by one of them and give it a try, but don't hesitate to design your own experiment. You have agency in your own life to take steps to pass through. Experimenting your way into a new reality is a great expansion plan as your mind and heart grow.[2]

Damned If We Do, Damned If We Doubt

*Sometimes this has left me groping in the
darkness, hoping in the darkness, I will
run into you again. . . . I'll wait for your
mystery to rise up and lead me home.*
—Sara Groves, "Mystery"

I got my first pair of glasses when I was in second grade. My eyes have been getting progressively worse since then, and at this point I am useless without glasses or contacts. Before I go to sleep at night, I've made it my habit to put my glasses on my nightstand next to my bed. More often than I would like to admit, I make the mistake of leaving my glasses somewhere else before I go to sleep. Like on my dresser or in the bathroom. This results in mass confusion when I wake up.

I am whatever the opposite of a morning person is. I wake up and hate life for at least half an hour. It's rough for anyone who has to be in my presence during that time. In my groggy, already-ticked-off-at-morning state, I feel around for my glasses, and if they aren't where they are supposed to be, what usually comes out of my mouth is the phrase, "Hey! Who moved my glasses?!"

This, of course, is a ridiculous question, as though my husband or the dog moved them while I was sleeping. My husband says nothing because he is a smart man. And because he knows that Morning Steph is not a nice person.

Clearly no one took my glasses. They just aren't exactly where I expected them to be. But they *are* somewhere. They are not far from me, but it feels like they have disappeared. This is how so many people feel as they wake up to the reality that they are doubting their faith in God. They reach out for where they thought they had left God. But they feel nothing! In those moments, it's easy to have the knee-jerk response, "Hey! Who moved my Jesus?"

This can be the beginning of doubt and questions that may grow to consume your heart. It feels as though God has moved or changed, leaving you wondering if Jesus is who he said he was. You can easily wonder if what you've been taught about

God is true—and how could you know? You begin to frantically search, unable to see clearly enough to grasp onto God or to see where God might have gone.

To make matters worse, many in the Christian tradition pour salt on the wound in these moments. A pervasive and harmful teaching equates doubt to a sin or sees doubt as a sign that someone is weak. I don't think doubt is sinful or weak, and my hunch is that these perspectives come from a misunderstanding of just a few passages of the Bible.

Waves Tossed in the Wind

When reading through the narrative of the Bible, we are reminded again and again that humans have always struggled through doubt and questions about God. Jacob wrestled with God all night long in Genesis.[1] The Hebrew people experienced doubt throughout the Old Testament. When they didn't seem to get what they wanted from God, they asked lots of questions and expressed doubts and even anger at God. In the Psalms, we see the song writer express questions like this from Psalm 13, "How long, Lord? Will you forget me forever? How long will you hide your face from me?"

Even Jesus's followers struggled with doubt while he was with them. The father in Mark 9 who wanted his son to be healed said the now-famous line, "I believe, help me overcome my unbelief!" Peter doubted—as Jesus invited him to walk on water, Peter began to sink.[2] Thomas doubted Jesus so distinctly after the resurrection that popular culture has given him the nickname "doubting Thomas."[3] He wanted Jesus to *prove* that he was really alive after his resurrection. But it's not like Thomas was the only one; most of Jesus's followers doubted that he had come back to life. These stories are comforting to me. Jesus always engages those who doubt with love and tries to help them deepen their understanding.

For some reason, many Christian leaders and pastors have overlooked these stories and defaulted to just a few passages that seem to contradict the Bible's openness to doubt. This has left many feeling they are damned if they doubt rather than encouraged to be honest with their questions. Barna studies have shown that at least two-thirds of those who self-identify as a Christian, or who have in the past, experience doubt in their life of faith.[4] Yet many who experience doubt feel a deep sense of shame. When we experience doubt, most of us are very unlikely to bring those doubts and questions to spiritual leaders. People in roles like mine either don't teach on the subject of doubt or teach with a bad biblical hermeneutic that interprets the original intent of the biblical writer incorrectly.[5]

For instance, one of the most damning passages used is James 1:6–8 (NIV):

> But when you ask, you must believe and not doubt, because the one who doubts is like a wave of the sea, blown and tossed by the wind. That person should not expect to receive anything from the Lord. Such a person is double-minded and unstable in all they do.

The Greek word used in this passage for *doubt* is *diakrinoe*, meaning "to withdraw or desert, to separate oneself in a hostile spirit or enmity in separation." When this word is used other places in the Bible, it describes the separation and enmity between the Jews and gentiles. Or when the archangel Michael is said to be "standing against" Satan.[6] Yet, look at how our most popular Bible translations render the word here:

- New International Version (NIV): "not doubt"
- New Revised Standard Version (NRSV): "never doubting"
- King James Version (KJV): "nothing wavering"
- New American Standard Bible (NASB): "without any doubting"

Based on these translations, it's no wonder we assume James is saying, "If you ever question or doubt God, you will be a wave tossed by the wind. God won't give you anything, and you will be unstable in all you do."

A more accurate translation of *diakrinoe* would be: "If you separate yourself from God and are against God or hostile toward God in your life, you are like a wave tossed by the wind."

This exegesis focusing on the original language helps us reflect on the message that James had for the original audience.[7] A helpful hermeneutic for us today would be to think about our lives and to ask whether we are hostile or against God. If so, then James is referring to us. If we are questioning, doubting, or even angry with God (as we see the psalmist lament over and over), we are not the kind of person James is referring to.

When Peter doubts and falls into the water, Jesus says, "why do you doubt?" The Greek word used is *distazo*, which is the word in Greek most similar to our English word *doubt*. It means literally "to doubt or waver." But even as Jesus names Peter a doubter, he doesn't say, "Peter, you are unstable in all you do! You are a wave tossed in the wind." Instead, Jesus calms the storm.

In the "doubting Thomas" story, the word translated as *unbelief* in the NIV is *apistos*, which means "not able to trust." Jesus responds by letting Thomas touch his wounds, and that increases trust for Thomas.

It's so clear in these stories that Jesus moves toward the doubters, not away.

Doubting and wavering do not cause God to abandon or judge the questioner. God invites us to press into our doubts and questions when we see the surprising results for those who engage in this challenging process.

Barna's 2017 study revealed that 12 percent of people who acknowledge a time of spiritual doubt in the past lost their faith, 7 percent said their faith weakened, 28 percent experienced no change in their faith, and 53 percent said it strengthened their relationship to God. So overall, 81 percent of those studied said their faith did not change or was stronger after going brick by brick through the wall of doubt.

These findings help me to lean on the promises from God in Scripture, like this one from the prophet Jeremiah: "You will seek me and find me when you seek me with all your heart."[8] "Seeking with all of your heart" is active and probably takes a lot of emotional strength and perseverance. But these studies suggest Jeremiah's promise from God was true! Jeremiah was writing to people in exile—people in a wilderness generation—and telling them to keep seeking God with all their heart. Sounds applicable to me!

The Bible warns us about what happens when people become hard hearted.[9] They are not able to hear from God or find God. Our hearts can harden easily when we hit the wall. When this collision happens repeatedly, a callus can easily form. But our hearts don't have to stay that way. When we recognize how Jesus responded to those who were doubting, we just might begin to accept his compassion. And that can help us soften our hearts once again. Perhaps, we can have some compassion for ourselves as well.

Think about the analogy of a heart. It's a muscle with an important job. Unhealthy lifestyles cause the heart to experience calcification. It literally gets harder as its muscle tissue turns to bone. So the hardness of the heart doesn't lead to strength but makes the heart weaker. We think of hard and strong as a pair, just like weak and soft. When we seek with all our heart, it's healthy and strengthened and we avoid dangerous hardening.

Moving from Skeptic to Seeker

When Jeremiah wrote the letter to those in exile, encouraging them to seek God with all their heart, he wasn't asking them to do something easy. To truly seek, we have to move away from skepticism. I think there is an inner skeptic in all of us. It is that voice that tells us to be cautious and careful not to trust where trust has not been earned. At times, it serves us well and helps us avoid those who mean to do us harm. I know my inner skeptic will always be with me. But to seek after something with all of your heart, you have to set aside your inner skeptic and embrace a posture of openness. I mentioned in an earlier chapter that we need to move from knowing to seeking. Most of us take a detour through skepticism with a posture of questioning that presumes there are no answers that can be trusted, even before any are suggested.

Skepticism is in the same genre of life as uncertainty, but it is the sad, snarky side of the spectrum. Moving away from skepticism doesn't mean abandoning questions; it means genuinely wanting to know the answers. It doesn't mean pretending you believe something that you are unsure of; it means choosing to commit to a process even though you are uncertain what the outcome will be. Cynicism is often perceived as a move away from the black-and-white nature of certainty, but in reality, it's a form of false certainty. The cynic easily disregards certain situations, people, or worldviews because they have decided they know what is true and their judgment must be accurate.

Moving away from skepticism and cynicism to become a curious seeker softens and strengthens your heart.

Not Far from Any One of Us

The apostle Paul, during the days where the church was still just beginning, spoke to a group of people who were not yet Jesus followers in the city of Athens, a city with many different gods. He walked out into an open area surrounded by idol statues made of stone and other adornments. And he said to all the people gathered there:

> The God who made the world and everything in it is the Lord of heaven and earth and does not live in temples built by human hands. And he is not served by human hands, as if he needed anything. Rather, he himself gives everyone life and breath and everything else. From one man he made all the nations, that they should inhabit the whole earth; and he marked out their appointed times in history and the boundaries of their lands. God did this so that they would seek him and perhaps reach out for him and find him, though he is not far from any one of us. For "in him we live and move and have our being."[10]

Paul was speaking to the skeptic in all of them—the little voice that caused them to make one idol after another so that they could be sure they were covering their bases. Paul acknowledged their desire to be able to reach out and touch a god. These stone gods were static and unchanging. They weren't active, so they wouldn't move overnight while the people were sleeping, causing them to wake up asking, "Who moved my idol?!" Paul understood this, and so do I. I wish I could reach out and touch God physically.

But Paul said to these people, "God is more than stone! God gives you your very breath, God put you where you are, where you live, where you work, for a reason: so that you would seek God and find God, because God is not far from any one of us."

God doesn't change, but God does move. And *we* change and move, too.

Sometimes we reach out for God and don't find God in the same place as before. We don't connect with God like we used to.

But it's a mistake to assume that this means that God is not near. It might mean you have expanded and changed, and when that happens to you, it changes all of your relationships, doesn't it?

Paul says God wants people to "seek him and perhaps reach out for him and find him, he is not far from any one of us."

This is a call to be active: to seek, to reach out, to find. Don't stop looking until you touch something or see something that feels like it might be God. And when you feel the tips of your fingers brush against something holy, move toward it.

Because even if you're doubting, Jesus is not running from you but rather wants you to follow.

The following are some experiments you could try in order to "pass through" from skeptic to seeker.

Questions and Doubts Inventory

Take out a journal or start a new document on your computer and write out every question and doubt that has been on your mind and heart. Next, take some time to meditate on the level of importance each question has to you in your life. Put an asterisk by three or four of the questions that seem most important to you.

Meditate on the following:

- Why are these questions so important to you?
- What is at stake if you don't find a sufficient answer to each question?
- What would finding answers to these questions change about how you live your life?

Find a conversation partner and talk through what you discovered in this experiment.

Visio Divina

The Latin phrase *visio divina* means *divine seeing*, and it shares roots with the ancient practice of *lectio divina*, which means *divine reading* (this experiment will be offered in a future chapter). This experiment could work with many different images, but I've used Rembrandt's *The Return of the Prodigal Son*. Google the image, and then try to look at it with the highest resolution quality possible. This painting depicts the story Jesus tells a group of people who were often marginalized and judged (you can find it in Luke 15:11–32).[11]

As you gaze at the painting, meditate on the following:

- What do you notice about each character in the painting?
- What significance would you give to the appearance and the clothing of each character?
- Why did Rembrandt paint the father with what appears to be one larger masculine hand and one smaller and more tender hand?
- What other observations would you make of the father in this painting, who represents the God figure?

Finally, spend a significant amount of time wondering about this question:

- Can I believe that a God like this truly exists? Try your best to listen to the deepest part of yourself and be open to listening to the voice of the Divine.

Find a conversation partner and talk through what you discovered in this experiment.

Dwelling and Seeking Map[12]

Take out a sheet of paper and draw a circle using dashed lines in the middle of the page, about the size of a large orange. Next, draw a circle outside the first circle that can reach to the edge of your sheet of paper; this line can be a solid line. Leaving plenty of space to write in each circle, label the inner circle *dwelling* and the outer circle *seeking*. Now get another sheet of paper and draw the exact same diagram.

Dwelling represents the truths in your life that feel settled and comforting. They represent where you feel at home in your mind and heart. The *seeking* outer circle represents the awakening anxieties, questions, doubts, and curiosity you are experiencing.

If you can, consider a time when you were experiencing less feelings of doubt or confusion than you do today. Write the year on the top of that page. Jot down bullet points in the inner circle that represent the dwelling areas of your life at that time and in the outer circle add bullet points that represent the seeking areas of your life at that time. Write the current year at the top of the other sheet of paper. Do the same exercise for how you feel about dwelling and seeking today.

After you have completed the exercise, meditate on these questions:

- What initial observations do you have about what has changed?

- Can you imagine a time when some of the seeking aspects of life might return to the dwelling circle?
- What is still in the dwelling circle? Have those things given you the needed comfort to sustain you through the seeking? How can you move toward those aspects of life in order to be encouraged?
- What aspects of the seeking circle are you actively pursuing in order to discover and expand? What aspect are you avoiding and why?
- How many years are there between the two maps? Use your imagination to wonder about how the map would change that same number of years into the future.

Find a conversation partner and talk through what you discovered in this experiment.

The Bags We Carry

We cannot selectively numb emotions,
when we numb the painful emotions,
we also numb the positive emotions.
Vulnerability sounds like truth
and feels like courage. Truth and
courage aren't always comfortable,
but they're never weakness.
—Brené Brown

I sat staring at the Thomas Kinkade knock-off painting in my therapist's office. My eyes always trace the lines of the old farmhouse whenever I am struggling to fully grasp the reality of what my therapist is helping me to unearth deep in my soul. He is good at helping me bring to the surface emotions that are difficult for me to access. For the last few months, I had been working through a heaviness and fatigue that he had helped me name as a low-grade depression called *dysthymia*.

"Steph, you've been carrying around so many wounds and emotions that you picked up along the way through life experiences. Imagine you are wearing a full backpack and are carrying a heavy suitcase in each hand. If you go through your life that way, you are bound to get slowed down. Your mind and your heart are slowing down because it's just too much to carry."

"It's just too much to carry." This sentence echoed in my mind.

I had a hard time reckoning with my diagnosis of depression. Those in a helping profession—spending most days thinking about the emotional needs of those they serve—tend to spend less time tending to their own emotional needs. As a pastor, I know other spiritual leaders, as well as social workers, teachers, doctors, and others who had come to the same realization: I am carrying too much, and I can't go on like this. Therapists are a gift to the church! Just like teachers and administrators, therapists deserve their own appreciation day with cards and memes and gifts. Remember to thank your therapist today—or consider finding a therapist! We all can benefit from their work.

I am so thankful that I was able to process the weight of all I was carrying around before it caused greater damage. I'm sure some of you reading this have experienced firsthand the crippling effects of major depression and anxiety. Mental illness can't all be traced back to specific life experiences, and I would never want to blame "life baggage" for all we struggle with. But as my therapist and I worked through the heaviness I felt, we were able to name the baggage I was carrying, and that was the first step in being able to figure out how I could start "traveling light" rather than lugging everything with me.

I had no idea how much baggage I was carrying from holding my dad's hand as he took his last breath in my senior year of high school. I didn't realize I had picked up so much extra weight from some of the bizarre things my youth pastors and their undertrained interns said to me. I didn't know the depression my friend wrestled with in high school had affected my trust in God so severely. Some of the hurtful words I heard from people I worked with were like bricks in a bag on my back. This and so much more had to be unpacked one bag at a time.

Even if you haven't dealt with depression or anxiety, you are carrying baggage. We all carry baggage; I have never met someone who didn't have any. Of course, I know a lot of people who don't believe they're carrying any baggage. Trust me, they are, and so are you. Baggage is a part of life. We bring the experiences we've had with us into our present and into our future. The question is, do we need all that we are carrying to go with us? Once we realize the answer to that question is "no," we can begin to travel light.

When I ask people what led them to doubt or question their faith, nearly everyone points to something they experienced in life. That might seem obvious. But remember the Wesleyan Quadrilateral from chapter 5: Scripture, tradition, reason, and experience make up the four sources that inform our faith. Some people name qualms with the Bible or with the tradition and history of Christianity as why they began to doubt. There are a handful of people who have told me that reason has led to their questions—usually highly intellectual people who appreciate philosophy and deep questions. But *most* people talk about an experience that caused them to question and doubt their faith. Only after this experience did they begin to ask questions in the arenas of Scripture, reason, and tradition.

Experiences that trip the doubt wire vary: being told that real Christians just believe and don't ask questions, religious leaders that fail you or cause spiritual abuse, physical or emotional abuse by someone you trusted, betrayal by close friends or partners, chronic illness, cancer, car accidents, miscarriage, death and loss, suffering of all kinds, confusion when the church doesn't care for the marginalized, the hypocrisy of Christians, people using the Bible as a justification to hurt or oppress others, seemingly unanswered prayers, loss of a dream you thought God had given you.

I could fill pages upon pages with stories that I have heard over the years about experiences like these. You are all so brave for having shared those experiences with me. Whenever I hear from courageous people like you, whether it is through an email or social media, a time of prayer after a worship service or over a cup of coffee at a local coffee shop, I am instantly standing on holy ground. Spending time in that space with so many people has shown me that we are all carrying baggage that needs to be unpacked if we are going to move forward in freedom. A few categories of baggage have emerged as themes in your stories. There is a chance that unpacking the bags could cause more doubts and questions, but it is absolutely worth it.

Relational Baggage

The relationships in which I experienced betrayal created the heaviest baggage in my life. No healthy person is unaffected by betrayal, but I have learned that my personality type has a specific aversion to betrayal, and a deep fear of it. So when I experience what feels like a betrayal, it affects me deeply. It's my worst fear coming true before my eyes. Growing up in the church, I heard a lot of sermons about how we are not supposed to sin but few about what to do when you are the one who is sinned against. Being sinned against leads to some of the heaviest baggage.

When one of my best friends met her husband, I got along with him right away. He really made her happy, and I enjoyed spending time with them and our other friends. They helped in the beginning stages of the church plant that became the church I currently lead. I was one of the first to know when they got pregnant with their daughter.

So you can imagine the betrayal I felt when a few days after their daughter's first birthday, my friend's husband told her, and then me, that he had been having an affair for a year. Clearly, the deepest betrayal was to my friend. But I had trusted him with her. I had trusted him with leadership within my church. I had trusted him as a friend! Though she was willing to work through the pain to try to save their marriage, he just couldn't do it. I came to a place of understanding that we are all broken people, and he was no different. It doesn't excuse what he chose to do, but I can find compassion for him as a brother. My best friend had been through the ringer, but she has since thrived as a person, a mom, and an educator.

The feelings surrounding that betrayal came roaring to the surface yet again when I found myself in a serious relationship a few years later. The man I was dating at the time told me he loved me, he told me the plans he had for our future together, he told me he'd try to make it work for him to stay in Minneapolis when it would be better for his career if he made a move. What he failed to tell me was that he was an alcoholic and had been for fifteen years. His alcoholism left a trail of failed relationships that he had told me fell apart for other reasons.

Nearly a year in, and I found out this shocking information. I did the thing you always do and retraced the last few months in my mind. Could I have seen this coming? He was so closeted in his drinking that there was no way I would have known. Once again, I believe God led me through a process of forgiveness. After countless conversations, I was able to forgive him, but it wasn't enough for the relationship to survive. His own process was just too heavy to carry and also be in a relationship. He had just begun to be honest with himself that he had a disease called addiction, and there was a long road ahead that he needed to start to walk down on his own.

We have all picked up a lot of relational baggage along the way. Relational baggage can come from our family of origin, even our cultures. It can come from friends and partners, from leaders and mentors.

No amount of compassion or forgiveness in my heart can completely take away the weight that these experiences have put on my shoulders. However, choosing to work through the trauma has lightened the load. Being honest about how these betrayals affected me has given me a freedom that didn't seem possible when I was in the midst of them.

Church Baggage

Anyone who has spent any time in the church has church baggage. There's no question—we all do. My bags started to get packed full at a young age. When I was nine years old, I was at my friend's summer lake cabin in Wisconsin. A news special came on the TV, and much to my surprise, on the screen was my church building.

"Is that your church?" my friend's mom asked me. They were Catholic, so my friend Linda and I had a lot of conversations about our extremely different experiences of our faith communities.

It was my church. I watched in horror and disbelief as the news program took an hour to detail the scandal that had rocked this suburban church community just three years prior. The pastor was arrested and convicted on more than twenty accounts of child molestation over the thirty years he had been the pastor. He was currently serving time in prison, and the story was documenting those who had come forward to tell their story in hopes it would empower others to get help. I now know how common clergy sex abuse and sex scandals are in this country—a horrifying reality.

I had no idea that this had happened three years prior in my church. I knew the pastor had left, and I remembered the nine months my dad filled in as a temporary preacher. I remembered when our new pastor began to lead, but I had had no idea what prompted all this change.

I was six years old at the time, so it isn't surprising that my parents hadn't given me the details. As a nine-year-old, I was beside myself with emotion. We returned home from the cabin that night, and I remember being lost in my thoughts as we drove. What does this mean? Why would my parents hide this from me? Did they lie to me? What else is a lie? How can I trust this new pastor if the other one is now in prison? If I can't trust the pastor, can I trust my Sunday-school teacher? Can I trust my church? Can I trust *any* church?

The number of items that ended up in my church baggage in just that one day I will never completely know. But what I do know is that pretending I'm not carrying the weight, or that it isn't heavy, doesn't work. Especially now that I lead a church myself. Very little that anyone could tell me about an experience they have had at a church would shock me.

Some have asked how I can continue to lead a church when I have seen the dark and seedy underbelly of what is supposed to be the bride of Christ. But, hearing the pain others have experienced at the hands of the church is precisely what motivates me to follow God's leadership to try to create spaces where people can have a different experience with the church. Yet, I know that my actions as a leader have created church baggage in the lives of others—this is unavoidable. My dad always made the joke, "When you find the perfect church, it won't be perfect anymore, because now you'll be there." It was his way of saying we are all broken people. Any gathering of humans is going to be full of brokenness because people are full of brokenness. The Christian hope that I hold onto, on the days when I do have faith, is that brokenness isn't the end of the story that God is telling!

The other reason that I am able to continue to lead in the church is because I carefully unpack the baggage that I inevitably carry. I know that I will continue to discover more about my baggage and how it shapes me. More is added to my bags all the time, and I have to continually examine them. Throughout my journey, I need to stop and see what I've picked up along the way. Talking to other people about it has lightened the load and kept the contents of the baggage and the resulting trust issues from exploding all over my friends, or worse my congregation. The baggage has shaped me, but that doesn't mean I have to carry all of it forever.

Baggage from Loss and Suffering

We all carry baggage from loss and suffering. Our relational and church baggage can lead to loss and suffering. But we also encounter countless other experiences of loss, pain, and brokenness in life. Sometimes it is our own pain and suffering, or the suffering or loss of someone close to us. In these times of pain and grief, I hold on to Jesus's statement that God is close to the brokenhearted. It just doesn't always *feel* that way.

No words can fully express the depth of sorrow, anger, and anguish that comes from experiencing suffering. The late theologian James Cone said, "Suffering naturally gives rise to doubt. How can one believe in God in the face of such horrendous suffering as slavery, segregation, and the lynching tree? Under these circumstances, doubt is not a denial but an integral part of faith. It keeps faith from being sure of itself. But doubt does not have the final word. The final word is faith giving rise to hope."[1]

When I need words to express this type of pain, I turn again and again to the lament psalms. Found in the book of

Psalms, right in the middle of the Bible, lament psalms are full of expressions of sadness, sorrow, and grief. Yet nearly all of them end with the hope Cone describes that rises from faith. These are psalms that are dominated by expressions of anger and frustration. Here are two examples:

My soul is in deep anguish.
    How long, Lord, how long?
Turn, Lord, and deliver me;
    save me because of your unfailing love.
Among the dead no one proclaims your name.
    Who praises you from the grave?
I am worn out from my groaning.
Psalm 6:3–6

Save me, O God,
    for the waters have come up to my neck.
I sink in the miry depths,
    where there is no foothold.
I have come into the deep waters;
    the floods engulf me.
I am worn out calling for help;
    my throat is parched.
My eyes fail,
    looking for my God.
Those who hate me without reason
    outnumber the hairs of my head;

many are my enemies without cause,
    those who seek to destroy me.
I am forced to restore
    what I did not steal.
Psalm 69:1–3

Professor of clinical psychology Dr. Julie Exline has conducted a number of studies on prayer that show people are very hesitant to admit their feelings of anger toward God. That kind of openness is just too scary for some people. She says that people tend to "describe a sense of spiritual dryness when they are actually suppressing that anger."[2] Perhaps the anger is a wedge between the person and God, just like it would be between that person and a friend or family member. It's worth wondering what holds us back from expressing our anger. It can be different reasons depending on your experience.

Generally speaking, dominant culture tends to encourage the suppression of anger, especially for women and people of color. The thought that a woman or person of color who is angry is "crazy" is pervasive. This is one of the reasons we hold back in expressing our anger to God. The irony is that other people are affected when we express the anger we feel, but God is not. Yet, there is still a pervasive fear of being honest with God when people feel angry. The ability to lament and to express anger to God about the world or toward God can be very healthy and lead to healing. We'll talk more about this in chapter 13.

There are no easy answers to the problem of evil—why a good God lets evil things happen. Volumes and volumes have been written by humans trying to wrestle through this concept. But what I do know is that God isn't afraid of our questions or our anger and frustration. The psalms teach us that God welcomes our sorrow, anguish, fear, and anger. Other humans tend to have a harder time when we express these emotions, but we shouldn't let the reactions of other people dictate our god concept. God's love is big enough to encompass our suffering—and even our anger.

Jonathan Martin wrote about what it feels like to go through deep pain, as though you were a ship that got wrecked on the sea of life. He talks about what it's like on the other side of the shipwrecks of life. "From this new-found capacity for pain, for sorrow, for torment, for agony, for endless waves of grief, comes the biggest surprise of them all—your new-found capacity for joy. You did not know you could suffer so intensely. Neither did you know you could experience joy this intensely."[3]

Unpacking the Bags

Some of the baggage you've carried with you doesn't need to come with you any longer. I work with my therapist, or a conversation partner or friend, to help discern what I can take out of my bag and leave behind. This is hard work, just like when you realize that you've overpacked for a trip. It is difficult to discern what is truly needed and what can be left behind. If you are very honest, you might find you have taken on a false narrative: "I need to take this experience with me so that I don't get hurt like this again" or "I am carrying the weight of this experience because I deserve the shame it's caused, and it is a form of penance to carry it every day." We all end up with some stowaways in our baggage that we didn't even realize had joined the journey uninvited.

When the baggage you've been carrying becomes too heavy, it's not time to worry. It's time to set those bags down and figure out what's inside them. We can't ignore them or pretend that they don't exist. Our baggage has significantly shaped our ideas about God, the church, the world, and ourselves.

When we carry our bags for a long time, we may not realize how many of the contents are no longer useful. By being willing to set them down, we offer ourselves the opportunity to lighten the load. The extra weight can lead to curiosity fatigue and can strip us of our sense of wonder. Even worse, it can keep us from being a part of the change we want to see around us. When we are fatigued, we aren't able to look outside ourselves and see those suffering or in need of love and acceptance. When we hold *all* our baggage, we don't have a free hand to extend to our neighbor. To move forward, we will have to examine the contents of our bags.

Here are some experiments you can try as you work to move from weighed down to packing light.

Divine Sightings

Take a journal or notebook and place it next to your bed. Every night for a week do the following: Draw a line down the middle of the page. On one side write "find the good" or FTG. On the other side write "notice the negative" or NTN. Then, think through your entire day and list on the FTG side anything that seemed to you like it was good: a positive aspect of God or Jesus, something that made you feel joy, happiness, depth of meaning, a focus on those outside of yourself, or like you were expanding. On the NTN side, write anything that made you feel negative, anxious, depressed, meaningless, inward, or like you were shrinking.

After a week of doing this, look through the pages and meditate on these questions:

- What themes do you observe?
- Notice what sticks out as unusual compared to the rest of the week, on either side, and wonder what circumstances led to that experience.
- What role, if any, do you think God played in the experiences of either column?
- Did you notice something that could possibly be God's presence in the midst of any of the experiences mentioned? If so, at any time did it seem like you were specifically close to or far from God?

Consider doing this experiment again for a week after a month or two to compare the experiences.

Find a conversation partner and talk through what you discovered in this experiment.

Family Baggage Tree

This might seem like a negative experiment to try, but we must realize that the bags we carry are often full early in life because of our family of origin. Consider this experiment as a way to take stock of the ramifications of the baggage that was handed to us by the people in our families. Be sure to hold this with grace, as most baggage is given to us unintentionally. This baggage can be passed through genetics but also from the environment, so this practice works for those who are adopted or who grew up primarily in a family that was not their birth family.

Use a sheet of paper or google "family tree template" in order to make a basic family tree. Start with your grandparents on both sides and then create the family tree including your parents, step-parents, siblings, step- or half-siblings, and then any spouses or kids your siblings may have. From there, add your aunts and uncles and cousins. Of course, a family tree can go much deeper than this, but for this exercise this will be sufficient.

After writing out your family tree, use a different-color pen or pencil to make little notes as you observe the following that you are aware of or suspect to be true:

- Marriages
- Divorce
- Separation
- Death
- Adoption
- Abortion
- Miscarriage
- Substance use
- Mental illness
- Physical illness
- Infidelity
- Unhealthy spirituality
- Domestic violence
- Sexual abuse
- Conflict
- Disengaged or cut off from the family
- Enmeshed or too attached to someone in the family
- Anything else that could contribute to baggage

Now pick a third color and make notes as you observe the following that you are aware of or suspect to be true:

- Healthy, empowering relationships
- People who have been empowering you
- Anyone who you see as a mentor
- Those who seem spiritually engaged in some way
- Those who seem fulfilled in their career

- Those who seem to be self-aware and able to advocate for themselves
- Those who have shown the ability to have healthy conflict
- Anything else that seems positive

Now meditate on the following questions:

- What patterns do you see in your family tree?
- Who seems to go against the patterns of your family tree and why?
- What aspects of these patterns do you see in your life, and how do you think they have impacted you both positively or negatively?
- What did you notice about your relationships?
- Who has most significantly influenced your life both positively and negatively?
- What about your relationships would you keep the same and what would you change?

Find a conversation partner and talk through what you discovered in this experiment. If you find these patterns to be very strong or stifling in your life, it is a great idea to process this map with a counselor or therapist.

Truth Beads

Go to a craft store or the craft section of a store and look for some string and at least seven beads. The beads should be as large as you can find and be able to be written on with a sharpie or pen. Next, sit down and brainstorm on a sheet of paper all the encouraging things you think might be true, even if they seem to fly in the face of some of your experiences in life. For instance, you may write "God is good" even though you have been through a very difficult season where bad things have happened that don't make sense. It's okay if they feel very simple, and don't be concerned if you notice how many things *cannot* go on this list of truths!

After you have made a list, try to put an asterisk by at least seven things that feel the truest to you in your life right now. Give them each a main word or small phrase so that you can represent the seven truths in some way on the beads. Next, tie the beads onto the string, leaving at least a few inches so you can move the beads from one side of the short string to the other. For at least a week, start and end your day saying each of your phrases, starting them with the words, "I believe . . ." and as you say each phrase, physically move that bead from one side of the string to the other.

When we have been through difficult situations in life, it gives us a script in our minds that literally rewires our brains. This exercise doesn't remove those negative experiences, but it helps to form new neural networks that can help you process even the difficult parts of your story from a place of encouragement that stems from your seven truths.

After a week, consider what that experience was like and if you feel any different emotionally or even physically after having started and finished your day with this experiment.

12

The Utopian Slope

Expectation is the root of all heartache.
—*Anonymous*

Nothing convinces you of the reality that all humans are broken and in need of grace than living with a group of people in a small space. Over a period of fifteen years, I was roommates or housemates with thirty-nine different people. I married my husband in my midthirties, which brought the total of different humans I had lived in close proximity with to forty. Each one of these beautifully complex people has shown me what brokenness looks like. I saw their brokenness up close and personal, and my own brokenness was revealed to me—I am not always an easy person to live with. I have learned so much from every person I have shared space with. In particular, I've learned that expectations are at the core of every conflict. We all have expectations for others, for ourselves, and for the experiences we have in life. It's only a matter of time before one or two—or ten—of those expectations come crashing down as we experience something completely different than we had anticipated.

Pastor Joseph Steinke calls these high expectations a *utopian hope*. As soon as I heard him use that phrase, I thought about the countless utopian hopes I have had over the years. Living with a group of people in community came to my mind right away! I had bought a house in the city, and six of my friends moved in. That meant there were seven women trying to live in one house with one fridge and only two bathrooms (not to mention the hyper dog). I remember thinking we would live together, pray together, and share what we had, and it would be a wonderful space for community and growth! It's like we would be living a modern-day experience of the community described in Acts. While that season in my life was wonderful in many ways, it turns out that living with that many women in a small amount of space—with a ton of opinions and all our issues—was really challenging. We learned how to do it well, but it was super-hard work.

Before that, I had utopian hopes about what college would be like, followed by seminary. Neither were what I expected. I had high expectations for what planting a church would be like and how easy it would be for my church to serve others in the neighborhood. I had no room for the idea of difficulty, hardship, or challenge in my utopian hopes for the church. It's been very difficult to serve a congregation and to serve our city. Nearly every day I wonder if we are doing this well and if all our efforts are making a difference.

Pastor Steinke has a name for coming down from our high expectations: the utopian slope. Sometimes the slope is slow and steady, like a child's slide. Other times you go down the slope like you're an Olympic skier on a steep headwall. Or perhaps it feels like you are thrust up and down and winding this way and that, as though you are on a roller coaster. Nearly everyone I talk to has some sort of utopian hope that has turned into a utopian slope. I am not sure what it is for you, it could be a job, marriage, having kids, grad school, traveling, starting your own business, the list could go on.

Going down the utopian slope is discouraging, and it influences our relationship with God and other people—especially when our utopian hope has been in the church or in a relationship with a pastor or mentor. When I was growing up, I lived through what are often called *mountaintop experiences*, when I felt like my utopian hope was really happening! Gathering with other Jesus followers felt like heaven was reaching down to touch the earth. In these times, God felt close enough that I could almost hear God whispering my name. Coming down from these mountaintop experiences felt like another kind of utopian slope. Right down into the valley.

Psalm 139 is one of the lament psalms I mentioned in the last chapter. In it, the psalmist prays:

> Where can I go from your Spirit? Where can I flee from your presence? If I go up to the heavens, you are there; if I make my bed in the depths, you are there.[1]

I think it's safe to say that the psalmist has experienced the descent of the utopian slope.

Shifting Metaphors

Thinking about our expectations as utopian hopes that are sometimes dashed—becoming utopian slopes—is a helpful metaphor. But we may need a bit more of a process-oriented illustration, so I'd like to suggest a new metaphor: LEGOs. Yes, the little bricks designed for children that some of us still build with on occasion (no shame!).

The experience I am about to describe can happen in any season of life, but I'll use college as an example because I've worked in that environment for fifteen years. I have had variations of this conversation on many occasions:

Student: I'm just struggling so much. It's like everything I thought I knew is crashing down around me. These classes are blowing my mind; my classmates had totally different experiences than I had in high school. We're reading books that say what seems like the opposite of what my pastor preached at my church back home. Not to mention all of the injustice I'm seeing now that I had no clue about growing up in the suburbs. I'm just so confused.

Me: Man, what you're going through is super-hard—but it's totally normal. It means you're doing a great job of beginning to think critically and taking personal responsibility for your life and your faith. You didn't think #adulting was just about learning to pay your car insurance or eat your vegetables, did you?

Student: Well, no, but when I thought about coming to a Christian college, I just thought it would be different. I thought it would feel like hanging out with my best friends, having a blast, learning about Jesus, and figuring out what I wanted to do with my life by taking interesting classes.

Me: It's normal to have those expectations, but I think what you were picturing was more like the best week you ever had at Bible Camp, not a realistic expectation for the challenges college would bring.

Student: Haha. *(sarcastic laugh, not appreciating my jab)*

Me: Okay, here's a way to think about it. Imagine one of those green LEGO boards that you had when you were growing up. Now picture that your whole life, people have been placing LEGO bricks on your board. You also added some bricks, and you have been building a tower of sorts, stacking the bricks on top of each other. The bricks represent beliefs, concepts, and ideas. Things you have come to know as truths.

(Now that I have had this conversation so many times, I actually keep a LEGO board and LEGOs in my office at the

seminary. NOT to play with, just for the illustration . . . mostly. These students are typically nineteen or twenty, so when they imagine their LEGO board it seems full to them. They feel that they have learned and experienced so much! They will soon realize how much more life experience they will have, even in just the next few influential years.)

Me: By the time most people get to college, they have something that looks like a tower; they maybe even feel proud of and confident about their tower. The tower represents their worldview, or paradigm of understanding God, themselves, and the world. They assume that nothing could happen in this new environment to threaten the tower, especially because their whole lives have been built upon it. What happens pretty quickly, if they are paying attention, is that the tower becomes less stable. Perhaps it leans significantly to one side and some of the bricks seem oddly placed. Classes like the one you mentioned cause them to wonder how some of the bricks even got there. It feels like the professor is pointing at your haphazard tower, almost forcing you to remove one brick after another—it can be embarrassing and terrifying.

Student: Yeah! That's totally what it feels like. No one else seems to be struggling like I am, but they probably can't see what I am going through either. I had never heard of some of the perspectives that were shared in class. I felt so dumb that I had come to think my perspective was the only one—even the right one. But now I'm not sure about anything anymore.

Me: Good! Even though uncertainty is challenging, you are thinking critically about your perspective. That helps you grow as a person.

Student: Well, my tower crashing down doesn't feel like growth.

Me: Totally, I get that. The tower coming down is a process we often call *deconstruction*, and when you do that, it feels like you are going backward rather than making progress. Often, the process of deconstruction happens slowly, but other times it's like someone smashed your tower in one fell swoop. The good news is, you can begin to reconstruct now that you have a clear LEGO board. You'll find that there are still some useful bricks left—cornerstone beliefs and concepts that you are able to build off of.

Student: It feels discouraging, like I'm starting over.

Me: But you aren't! The bricks are still sitting around your LEGO board for you to examine. This time, *you* get to decide if and how each brick gets placed. You can place a brick or two as you reconstruct your perspective and your faith. And you can then change your mind and take them off again. This is all a part of the process. The good news is that the structure that you rebuild will be much sturdier and able to hold firm under pressure. I hate to break it to you—your life will have some awesome experiences, but it will also have some really difficult storms. You'll want your new paradigm to hold up as you go through them.

Student: I know I know. I don't expect life to be easy all the time! *(rolls eyes at me)*

Me: Then you will see why it's important to be intentional and keep deconstructing and reconstructing. Some people get frustrated and shove their LEGO board away on a shelf to get dusty. Let's just say it doesn't go well for them. Before they know it, and without their input, another equally unstable tower is built. It's not easy to do this emotional, spiritual, and intellectual work. But most things that are important in life are challenging. The best advice I can give you is not to do this process alone. Let's brainstorm who the people are that you trust the most to share your journey with.

A few days after a conversation like this, I try to remember to stick one of those five-dollar LEGO sets in the student's post-office box with a note letting them know that I am praying for them. I have had to deconstruct and reconstruct my tower a number of times. I am increasingly comfortable with the reality that I feel *more* sure but about *fewer* things in life. Holding the tension of uncertainty has become easier as I do this work intentionally. We can grow in our capacity to hold tension when we practice and when others do this work with us.

From Confusion to Intention

This process I just illustrated goes beyond the utopian hope and the inevitable utopian slope and gives us a few more steps in the process. Alan Roxburgh, a researcher and professor, outlines the process of paradigm change:

1. Stability: Everything seems fine and sturdy. This is the time when the student in my example is happy with their goofy LEGO tower.
2. Discontinuity: The current way of seeing things begins to work less well. This is when the bricks are beginning to be plucked off of the student's tower one by one. The tower proves to be unstable, which brings about fear or worry.
3. Disembedding: The current perspective is just not holding up, and you begin to detach from it. This is when the student feels like they have taken nearly all their LEGO bricks off of their board, and they feel discouraged and disoriented.
4. Transition: The former perspective has been deconstructed, but a new way of seeing the world and God hasn't yet emerged. This is when the student notices that they still have bricks lying all around their board, and even some new bricks ready to be placed, but they haven't really begun to rebuild. This season can be very lonely and isolating.
5. Reformation: Beginning the rebuilding process in earnest. This is when the student realizes it's not an option to just leave the decimated tower; they must rebuild. This

time, as they build their tower, they do so with the intention to avoid things being placed haphazardly or by others without their participation. While the person doesn't want others to place their bricks *for* them, the healthiest reformers begin to choose a communal discernment process, which provides support and encouragement.

Anytime we undergo a change of paradigm, we go through a similar process. The question is not, Will our paradigms change? Rather the question is whether we will be *intentional* with the process or if we will just let it happen to us without engaging fully.

Here are some experiments that could help you move from confusion to intention when it comes to reconstructing.

Spiritual Timeline

Take a sheet of paper and turn it so you can write horizontally. Draw a line from one side to the other in the center of the page. On the left, write the year you were born, on the far right put an arrow because there is so much yet to come in your life.

Take time to go through year by year and write in any experience that you would consider spiritual in any way. For the sake of this experiment, consider this definition of spiritual: something that was a part of a religious ceremony or gathering, something that seemed to transcend the material or physical aspect of you and the world, and any time where you feel like you felt or experienced God.

After taking time to fill out your timeline, meditate on the following questions:

- What themes do you see in your spiritual timeline?
- Do you see the various experiences as connected in any way?
- Do you observe any utopian hope seasons or experiences? What contributed to the hope?
- Do you observe any utopian slope seasons or experiences? What contributed to the slope?
- Were there any experiences you would consider negative where you simultaneously felt close to or were experiencing God in some way?
- When you think about the future of your timeline, what are your hopes and what are your longings? (Hint: longing is often a sign that there is hope for the future, it's just more difficult emotionally than a more positive feeling of hope.)

Find a conversation partner and talk through what you discovered in this experiment. If thinking about these experiences makes you feel like the past has power over you or you feel stuck, it is a great idea to process this timeline with a counselor or therapist.

Lectio Divina

In Latin, this phrase means *divine reading*, and this ancient Christian practice can be followed with any passage of Scripture. For this exercise, here are two passages that are honest about the difficult aspects of a life of faith with others. The framework of the utopian hope and slope can be a guide for this listening: 2 Corinthians 4:7–12 and/or 2 Timothy 2:14–16. Here is an outline you can follow. If anything doesn't feel genuine to you, feel free to skip it. Try doing a practice like this once a day for a week to allow this experiment to lead to greater discovery and meaning.

Introductory Prayer

- Humbly recognize the loving presence of the Trinity: Father, Son, and Spirit.
- Praise and thank God for God's word and this moment of prayer.
- Ask the Holy Spirit for the gift to receive the word of God.

Lectio (Reading)

- What does the word of God say?
- Slowly read the passage a few times with attentive reverence, aloud if possible.
- Notice words that strike you in a particular way, positively or negatively.

Meditatio *(Meditation)*

- What does the word of God say to me?
- Dialogue with God about why those particular words or phrases struck you. How do they apply to you? What questions do you have for God about this?
- Reflect on your own reactions to the word. What is God showing you about yourself?
- Write down reflections and insights.

Oratio *(Praying)*

- What do I say to God in response to God's word?
- Respond sincerely in a conversation with God as with a friend; talk about what is really in your heart.
- Praise, thank, and trust God; ask for forgiveness; intercede, petition for graces.

Contemplatio *(Contemplation)*

- What conversion of heart is God asking of me?
- Be with the word and rest in God.
- Thank Jesus for living in and through me.

Concluding Prayer

- Praise and thank God for the graces received.
- Pray the Lord's Prayer.

Find a conversation partner and talk through what you discovered in this experiment.

Spiritual Practice of Simplicity

Often when we have experienced the descent from a utopian hope down a long utopian slope, we have to reckon with shattered expectations. When we have expectations of a grand experience or a significant transformation and those expectations aren't met, we are bogged down with all the what ifs and why nots. While those questions have their place, it can feel crowded in our minds and hearts. Choosing a practice of simplicity is an experiment that often helps people find clarity in their current situation. I suggest picking a reasonable time frame to start with for this practice. A month is usually a good starting point.

Take out your calendar and pull up your checking account. These two things give us the most insight as to what areas of life could use some simplicity. Ask the question, What might I prune or trim in my life to make space? Perhaps you are going to cut back on nights out or Netflix or take a break from a committee you are on. Additionally, you could choose not to spend money in a certain area this month, for instance on an often-purchased beverage or choosing to bring lunch to work rather than purchasing it.

Next, look at your physical spaces: home, office, car, and so on. Choose at least one space to deliberately simplify at least for a few weeks. For example, if you typically have a lot of piles, frames, or extra objects on your desk, remove them for a month of simplicity in that space.

Now that you've chosen to simplify some aspects of life, invite just one aspect to be added to the simplified space. Write down on a sheet of paper all of the things you feel your heart pulled toward, that you would consider wrong in the world around you. For instance, you might say that your heart goes out to those who are experiencing homelessness or people who are feeling isolated or lonely. Make a long list. Then choose just one area you could take action on in your life.

Finally, consider the following three ways to participate in this area: finances, time, and prayer. Let's use the passion for those experiencing homelessness as an example: First, financially invest in an organization supporting those without a home. Second, find at least two time frames when you can volunteer in a way that will give you direct relational experience with folks experiencing homelessness. Third, if you are in a season where you are able to pray, put a reminder in your phone or on your mirror to pray for this area of need.

Give financially, give time, and offer prayers.

This is an experiment that is really effective to do with a roommate, friend, or partner. Set an end date, and after it has passed, talk through what you experienced and discovered in this monthlong experiment.

Slay Your Dragon

Hope and Fear cannot occupy the same
space at the same time. Invite one to stay.
—Maya Angelou

One foot in front of the other, you're getting the hang of this journey now. You've passed through from skeptic to seeker, and you're committed to spending some time navigating the wilderness. You are doing your best to let wonder guide your feet rather than wandering aimlessly. The beginning of the trek was much more challenging before you realized you were carrying so much dead weight in your baggage. You off-loaded some of that baggage, and with just a lightly packed bag or two you are really picking up the pace. You are taking each step with intention, and you have left at least *some* of the confusion behind with the extra baggage.

As you ponder how you have expanded as a person thus far, you have a weird feeling that something is behind you. You turn your head around slowly to see nothing. A few more paces, and you still feel like you are being followed. You swear you hear something rustling in the grass. You feel your heart start to race, and this time you whip around sure you will find something on your heels. Nope, nothing again. A few moments pass by as your feet try to keep pace with your heartbeat. Now, not only do you have a sense that something is behind you, but you hear and then you feel something breathing down your neck! You start to run, only to make it a few yards before you trip over a branch on the ground. As you flip over you finally see what has been chasing you: a large, scale-covered, fire-breathing dragon! And if that weren't horrifying enough, you see that it has not only one but multiple flailing heads!

I use this image of a dragon to illustrate what it feels like to encounter grief, fear, and anger on our wilderness journeys. Not everyone encounters a dragon in the wilderness, and there are no two identical dragons, so the experience is unique for each of us. The important thing to know is that you can't out-run a dragon no matter how hard you try. Your only option is to turn around and face it. And then to slay your dragon one gnarly head at a time.

Grief

We often don't realize it when we are in the midst of grief and depression. I can't tell you how many conversations I have had where right in the middle of the conversation someone says something like, "Oh my gosh, I think what I am feeling is sadness. That's why I feel this way, I'm grieving!" There is no telling how long someone can go through life with the grief head of the dragon breathing its nasty fire-breath down their neck before they turn around and see their grief face to face. No wonder they are in pain! Grief is tricky like that.

Psychologists have taught us about the different stages of grief. Most studies show that the stages are not always linear and that people experience grief in many different ways. To move through grief, it's important that people feel freedom to express their sorrow in ways that make sense to them. Denial is often the first stage of grief, which is why so many of us don't realize we are grieving right away. "I'm not sad," we say, "what I went through really wasn't that bad." Peter Scazzero writes in his book *Emotionally Healthy Spirituality* about the many other defense mechanisms in addition to denial that we tend to implement to avoid the pain that comes with grief: blaming others, blaming yourself, rationalizing or offering excuses, intellectualizing or trying to let your brain do the work so you can avoid your emotions, and distracting or trying to find other things to occupy both your mind and heart.[1]

Scazzero says that grief and loss can "enlarge your soul." I love that image, and I have found it to be true in my own life. Enlargement is a form of expansion, which can lead us into a narrow place. I have found myself in narrow places where people weren't willing to engage with the grief I was facing. Perhaps you have experienced this as well. Grief is not something that you can avoid; you have to face it. The only way to slay this part of the dragon is to engage with the grief so you can move through it. No amount of self talk or picking yourself up by your bootstraps will lead you through grief. When we are going through it, we would rather be experiencing anything but grief; in our agony we'd love to experience whatever it is at the opposite end of grief! The problem is, the opposite end of grief isn't peace or happiness—it's denial. So being willing to face it is the only way forward.[2]

Scazzero uses the story of Job in the Bible as a model for how to move through grief. He suggests, as many scholars have, that Job represents all of us. While most of us don't lose everything all at once like Job does in the story, all of us will end life leaving everything behind. Scazzero outlines these stages for moving through grief:

1. Pay attention. Ask yourself about the emotions you are feeling and try to name them. We often have trouble expressing how we are feeling because when someone asks us "How are you?" we typically respond with the number-one lie in America, "I'm good!" At times that answer is true, but quite often everything is *not* good. I'm not advocating for oversharing when

someone is simply offering a benign greeting. But we need to start asking ourselves the deeper question: How am I, really?

2. Wait in the confusing in-between. Waiting is the woooorrrrst. No one likes waiting, and it is particularly difficult to feel like we are waiting on God—for a response to a prayer, for guidance, or for spiritual inspiration. But soul enlarging happens in the waiting. That's where capacity grows in our minds and hearts. God works in the midst of waiting in ways that we often overlook.

3. Embrace the gift of limits. We are finite human beings, and we therefore have limits. Your body, mind, talents, gifts, wealth, relationships, and time are all limited. If your limits are frustrating to you, know that I am with you. Whenever I hit my limits, I always try to squeeze in just a bit more. One of my friends said something that has stuck with me: "The end of myself is the beginning of Jesus." When I heard that, it was the first time I truly wanted to reach my limits—so that I could experience truly needing Jesus. When you are experiencing grief, you feel your limitations more readily. Embrace it.

4. Climb the ladder of humility. Scazzero uses a ladder to illustrate that humility is something that helps us rise even though we often consider humility to be something that lowers us. An unhealthy view of humility is to think about your limitations in order to make yourself lower than others. This ends up leading to a warped sense of self and as well as a disingenuous elevation of others. Instead, think of how realizing your limitations serves as a reality check that helps you engage humility.

My definition of humility is not thinking too little of yourself, or too much for that matter. Rather, it is to think of yourself accurately or with "sober judgment," as Paul talks about in Romans 12. Humility leads us to offer more compassion to ourselves and thus more compassion to others. As we grow in humility, we rise toward the top of the "ladder of humility," where Scazzero suggests we have the experience of "being transformed by the love of God."

5. Let the old birth the new. Beauty can be born out of the ashes, but it will take time. When something dies, it is really just the beginning of something new—think about the excitement of watching winter turn to spring each year. As Christians, we bear witness to the same sort of rebirth when we celebrate the resurrection of Jesus. When you turn to face whatever you're grieving (whether that be an actual death or a more figurative loss), you'll soon see that you can't go back to what used to be. You won't relate to God in the same way you did before, either. There is no such thing as "going back to the good old days." They weren't as good as they seem in hindsight anyway. When God leads us through grief, we are changed, often for the better.

Fear

Another head of the dragon for many is fear. Fear and anxiety are often listed together, and I think they are cousins more than synonyms. Anxiety is the term often used to diagnose what can be a crippling mental illness. When fear and anxiety begin to plague our lives on any scale, it most certainly feels like a dragon breathing fire down your back. It can be overwhelming to say the least. If you feel like your anxiety is too much for you to manage, don't hesitate to talk to a doctor or therapist. I know so many people that are so glad that they did. You don't have to live with the effects of chronic anxiety without support.

At the same time, all of us need to take stock of the way that fear and anxiety impact us. Recent findings suggest heightened anxiety is impacting nearly all of us. It's clear that anxiety is on the rise in American society as the American Psychiatric Association found a 5 percent increase of the National Anxiety Score in just one year between 2017 and 2018.[3]

For people who want to connect with God, fear is a significant problem. Many spiritual directors and guides suggest that fear is one of the core barriers between us and our relationship to God. Fear is a loud talker—like the voices in a crowded restaurant that drown out the conversation at your own table. Fear creates this kind of interference when we attempt to hear from God. I think this is why "don't be afraid" is said to God's people so often throughout the Bible. When God sends a messenger to the people, their first reaction is often fear. So the messenger exhorts, "do not be afraid" to calm the hearer and prepare them for God's message.

However, it isn't easy to turn off our fear. Pastors who preach about fear like it's a faucet you can just turn off have done more damage than good in this area. It's also important to note that chronic anxiety is often experienced by those who struggle with mental health. It is completely appropriate for therapy and medication to help in those occasions. It's completely inappropriate for someone to suggest to someone struggling with a mental illness that they need to "just pray more." In this chapter, I am focusing on the fear that is regularly experienced by everyone throughout life rather than the diagnosable illness.

Fear takes control of our motivations. For example, you may be motivated to live a life of radical generosity, giving of your time and finances to those who are in need. Fear sweeps in telling you to grip tighter to what you have, not to give it away. Financial caution seems like wisdom or common sense. But before you know it, your fear of not having enough is motivating you more than your value of generosity. That's just an example. I have seen fear motivate many to live in ways counter to their values.

Fear can be one of the most significant obstacles when trying to stay curious. Curiosity involves a desire to explore and discover. When you are fearful about what might be around the next corner, or behind the next door, you might avoid making those turns or opening those doors altogether. Fear causes containment and hinders expansion. It contains who you think you should be, who God is, and what your purposes might be in the world. The fear of the unknown holds you back from experiences and from opportunities. Fear holds you back when your mind and heart could be expanding, and you could be experiencing mystery and wonder. So what are the steps to move through fear and slay that head of the dragon?

1. Name your fears. You need to be honest and name what you are afraid of. Fear is a deep emotion; on the surface it could look like sadness, frustration, or apathy. Each of those emotions is valid, but it's worth digging deeper to see if the root of that emotion is fear. Sometimes you even need to dig to find the fear beneath your fear. It can be difficult to discover the actual root of the fear you are experiencing. For instance, I often fear that I am going to be misunderstood by those I am close to. But the fear beneath the fear is being abandoned, or worse, being betrayed by those I love. If they misunderstand my intentions, or my heart, they might leave me! It took a few counseling sessions to get to the core of that one, and it will take you time to dig to the root of your fears as well.

2. Summon courage. "Courage is not the absence of fear; it's moving forward even when you are afraid," or so goes the common platitude. Courage is something we access at the core of who we are deep in our hearts. We could swap "have courage" with "take heart." It is the willingness to name your fears, but also recognize that some things are more important than what you fear. What do you value that you won't live out if fear is your biggest motivator? Intentional integration and growth in your faith can be scary; curiosity is risky. People might be threatened or confused by the questions you are asking, and those questions will lead to change. Courage helps you name the deeper motivations in your life that are more powerful than

fear. For me, authentic relationships with people different from me is a high value. Especially people who have a different ethnic background. So I am going to take courage and step into friendships with people even though I will never be *fully* understood just as I seek to try to understand them and their life.

3. Take the next step. Once you can separate your fears from what you value, you can start to take steps toward what you value, even though you might still be afraid. The good news is, you only have to take one step at a time. You can make one connection with someone who can talk through your questions with you. Pick up that one book that piques your curiosity. Take one step toward learning about that career you may want to switch to. You don't have to take ten steps at once.

4. Keep up your fear radar. I wish the final step was to skip off into your life free from fear, but that just isn't reality. Fear is something we have to keep on our radar constantly. We can overcome specific fears, but we will never live free from fear altogether. So we have to stay diligent and constantly be aware of how fear is motivating us, because if we don't, it can begin to control our lives.

Anger

Ian Punnett wrote a really helpful book called *How to Pray When You're Pissed at God*. He says, "This permission to be real when angry is grounded in the traditional Judeo-Christian belief that humans have been given an array of emotions by

God." In the book, Punnett talks about a twelfth-century rabbi from Spain known as Maimonides. This rabbi believed that not only is anger an acceptable emotion but that you should always be able to access "just enough anger to have it never be said that you don't care about anything . . . if you aren't mad about something, you're probably not paying attention."[4] Anger leads to a sense of conviction that motivates us to act when we see injustice. Side note: some feel like we can't have conviction without certainty. I think we absolutely can! More on this in chapter 15.

When we experience pain, suffering, and loss in our own lives, we often feel that things are "not right." I would call that our core sense of justice or righteousness. Doing justice is working to make wrong things right. Our English words *righteousness* and *justice* are used to translate the same word in both biblical Greek and biblical Hebrew respectively. A helpful way to think of its meaning would be *rightness* or *right-making*. When we experience something that isn't right, our sense of justice rings an alarm and often triggers anger. We long for rightness, righteousness, or justice.

When I was seven years old, I found out my dad had a disease that was going to kill him. For a long time in my life, I wanted to pretend it didn't make me mad that I had to experience that as a little kid. But when a seven-year-old girl at my church found out her dad had degenerative MS, it made me mad! The suffering she and her family are going through made me angry. I realized that I was okay with being angry about what was not right in the lives of others, but I had been suppressing the anger I felt about my own experiences. Anger about the injustice we experience in our own lives and in the lives of others can eventually lead to compassion—for ourselves and for others. But when we suppress anger, or suggest that anger is not acceptable to God, we miss an opportunity to reach compassion.

The church is guilty of what I call *anger shaming*—trying to keep people from engaging that God-given emotion. For instance, I see this in the way that the white church has criticized black Christians for showing anger at the injustice and oppression they experience being black in America. "Angry black woman" is used as a derogatory phrase, as though these women have nothing to be angry about. If anger comes from experiencing what is not right, then this community absolutely has clear reasons for anger.

We need to embrace the anger inside of us and others and be encouraged to express it in healthy ways. A process to move through anger could look like this:

1. Name what is wrong. Anger often comes from a recognition that things are not right, and there is power in naming whatever that is. "It is wrong that a child should lose a parent while they are so young." "It's wrong that I have been treated in horrible ways because of the color of my skin." Sometimes you have to be honest about things that are wrong inside of you: "I'm angry

that I continue to lose patience with my kids. It's not right that I have such a short fuse." It seems counterintuitive, but it makes sense that we are angry about the things we feel like we continue to struggle with.

2. Discern what can be done. The serenity prayer by theologian Reinhold Niebuhr has become a foundational prayer for many. "God, grant me the serenity to accept the things I cannot change, the courage to change the things I can, and the wisdom to know the difference." Let your anger motivate you to change the things you are able to change. Nearly every important social change has been started by a "spark that became a flame," as civil-rights activist E. D. Nixon once said. That spark is often ignited by anger at what is wrong in the world. If you are angry because you feel like the church isn't angry *enough* at injustice, I'd say you're right. What can you do about that?

3. Surrender to your limitations. Not every wrong can be made right. That can paralyze us and keep us from trying. Our limitations—the fact that we can't fix everything—shouldn't hold us back from working to fix the things we can. This is where the serenity part of the prayer is so important. We can be honest with God when we are angry with God, others, or the world. Bringing those emotions to God gives us the opportunity to receive serenity, or peace. From a place of serenity, we are empowered to change what we can. If

we decide not to bring our emotions to God, then we don't have the same opportunity to receive.

4. Embrace compassion. One of the greatest gifts of anger at what is not right is that it can lead us to compassion. A simple definition for compassion is "concern for suffering." Anger can lead to a place of sensitivity, warmth, and love. If you are concerned for your own suffering, self-compassion is an expression of sensitivity and love with yourself. Many have said we can't truly show others compassion if we can't have compassion for ourselves. My god concept has led me to believe that God can get angry, because God is very concerned for the suffering. God is the only being that always moves anger toward compassion and love, and a relationship with God helps us do this as well.

Here are some experiments that help us move through grief, anger, and fear.

Intentional Mindfulness and Prayer

The practice of mindfulness involves intentionally focusing one's awareness on the present moment while calmly acknowledging and accepting one's feelings, thoughts, and physical sensations. We have been talking about how you need to turn around and face your dragons of grief, fear, and anger. To do this, you need to be willing to be present to these strong emotions and experiences. An experiment in mindfulness could help you to do this in a very tangible way.

This practice can take as little as five to ten minutes or can be extended as long as it's helpful.

- Find as quiet a location as possible.
- Sit in a comfortable posture and close your eyes.
- Focus on your breathing.
- Invite God to be with you in this process.
- Next, bring your awareness to your toes and the bottom of your feet.
- Then slowly scan your entire body as you notice any sensations you have.
  - There may be some pain.
  - Perhaps your hands are warm or cold.
  - Notice anything tingling or aching.
  - Pay attention to any part of your body that feels particularly heavy or light.
- If your mind wanders, gently bring your attention back to the process. Treat your mind like a puppy learning to sit. Be kind as you learn to focus your attention.
- Next, notice the emotions you are feeling. Invite the things that are deep to come to the surface so you can attend to them.
- Name the emotions you are feeling.
- Wonder if there are more that are beneath the initial feelings that you can access.

- Listen to see if there is anything God may be speaking to you.
- When you are ready to move, focus on the top of your head and notice the sensations as you did before.
- Move your attention through your whole body, ending with the bottom of your feet and your toes.
- Take your time moving on to the next activity of your day.

Find a conversation partner and talk through what you discovered in this experiment.

Honest Lament Poem

Laments are found throughout the Bible, specifically in Psalms and Lamentations. Psalms follow five parts:

1. Address to God—directing the lament toward God.
2. Lament to God—a very honest description of the issue, pain, suffering, or confusion the person is experiencing. The more honest and forthright, the better.
3. Confession of trust in God—a statement showing the belief that God will hear the prayer.
4. Request of God to act—very specific statements of what the person wants God to do.
5. Response of praise to God—portion of the lament where the person promises to offer praise and thanks

to God, believing that God is powerful enough to change their situation.

In a journal or piece of paper, you may follow these five steps and write out a lament in your own words. Many people prefer to use a lament psalm as a guide to inform the lament poem they are writing. You could even try to simply rewrite the lament in your own words. Hint: When you hear language about an enemy in Psalms, it is helpful to imagine the forces of evil that the enemy of God uses to bring about brokenness in our lives and the world. Psalm 85, 90, or 142 would be a good place to start.

Find a conversation partner and talk through what you discovered in this experiment.

Gratitude Meditation Prayer

As we've learned more about the brain, we can see that gratitude is an antidote to anxiety, anger, and fear. While it's important to face these emotions, when you are overwhelmed by them, this is a great experiment to try.

- Find a private space where you can lie down on a couch or bed.
- Set an alarm for thirty minutes to rest and even to nap.
- While trying to rest, envision being in the arms of God.
- Do whatever you can do to rest even if you don't fall asleep.

- When the alarm goes off, roll over on your stomach.
- Express as much gratefulness to God as you can think of.
- Don't get up until you have exhausted all gratitude.

Find a conversation partner and talk through what you discovered in this experiment.

14

Wrong Kind of Christian

May we be the ones who hold the doors open for others, who hold hands, who hold faces, who hold secrets for one another, who hold space for the pain and the brilliance, who hold the light and the salt, the complexity and the simplicity, the silence and the storm, the ones who hold our opinions loosely and yet love ferociously.
—Sarah Bessey

A number of years ago, I was asked to officiate a wedding for a couple in the bride's hometown of New Orleans, Louisiana. This just happens to be the hometown of my late father, who grew up in the city until he was eighteen. My dad was a pastor, as was his dad. I never met my grandpa, because he died before I had the chance. However, I have heard hours of stories about him, some that I am sure are myth and folklore. Nevertheless, all the stories taken together reveal that my grandpa and I were very different people. While we are both white, middle class, and Christian, the differences abound. We grew up in very different parts of the country, and we experienced American life in two very different generations. As I traveled from Minneapolis to New Orleans to officiate this wedding, my grandpa was on my mind.

The day of the wedding, I stopped by his grave site, where he is buried next to my grandma. As I stood there looking at his grave stone, a realization hit me: my grandpa would most likely not approve of the events of the weekend. Unable to ask him and know for sure, the details of the next twelve hours ran through my mind, and I wondered about how different his perspective would have been on each aspect of this day. First of all, I am a pastor who happens to be a woman. I'm pretty sure the idea that pastors must be male would have been on my grandpa's short list of theological certainties. The bride was African American, and the groom was European American. The groom had a Lutheran background, and the bride had a Pentecostal background. While the wedding was distinctly Christian and focused on Jesus, the couple served beer and had a toast with wine (kind of like the first story we hear of Jesus at a party in John 2:1–11).

I brought a lot of assumptions into this, but I had to imagine some of this scene would have met with his disapproval. As I thought through all of these realities, the phrase "turning in his grave" came to mind. I left the cemetery shortly after this realization, as the tension was just too great to consider while standing so near to where he was buried. I drove to the wedding venue (which was not a church—probably another ding from Grandpa against me that day) and thought about the significance of the different approaches two people in the same family can have when it comes to what it means to be a Jesus follower. One thing I know about my grandpa for sure is this: he spent his whole life trying to follow Jesus, just like I'm trying to do.

My story isn't unusual. Most of you are probably able to think of people in your immediate or extended family who are on a very different page when it comes to some of the conclusions you've made about what it means to be a person of faith. Perhaps you are just now asking questions that are leading you away from what your family or community has communicated as values or truths. It's normal for this to cause some anxiety. I never experienced this tension with my grandpa because I never knew him. However, there are others in my family and community with whom I have significantly different conclusions about what it looks like to follow Jesus, as well as very different interpretations of the same Scriptures. I fear we will take this anxiety as a sign that we are supposed to flee from these relationships or break them off in some sort of significant way.

When we feel this much tension, our fight-or-flight response can kick in. However, we can also choose the stress response of tend or befriend—and the latter is a better option. Boundaries are good and might be necessary for a healthy relationship moving forward, but totally dissociating from those with whom we have major differences of opinion can be detrimental as well. First of all, the cost of significant separation from these communities or relationships almost always means that some positive aspects of the relationship are also discarded. Second, being around people who think differently from us aids our expansion project with our minds and hearts. The echo chamber of agreement to what we already think can be very detrimental to our growth—spiritually, emotionally, and intellectually. I also see the opportunity when we stay in close relationship with those who think differently to continue to grow in their own perspectives. This doesn't always happen, but if we take ourselves and our own curiosity out of the equation, it's even more unlikely. When we are in relationship with others, we can encourage them to stay curious as well!

I have no idea what my relationship with my grandpa would be like if he had been around for the last thirty-five years to see one of his granddaughters grow up to follow in his vocational footsteps. From my experience connecting with other pastors who are also women, I know many stories of parents, grandparents, and siblings who began to rethink their perspective once there was a woman called to ministry in their family. When I told my grandma on my mother's side that I was going to seminary to be a pastor, she told me that women couldn't do that. I kindly told her I was going to do it anyway. I had studied the Bible and theology in depth to stand up for my position that the Bible affirms women in all roles in the church and society. I called her the next week and she proudly exclaimed, "I told my minister the good news that my granddaughter is also going to be a minister!" When I pointed out that she had had a different opinion just five days earlier, she said, "Well, that was before I knew I had a woman minister of my own!"

Brought to Complete Unity

Beyond the reasons already mentioned, one of the most important reasons we should try to make unity in diversity a priority is because it's what Jesus would do. It's not that Jesus wouldn't get into heated discussions and courageous conversations with those he disagreed with. We see Jesus do this all the time, especially with the religious leaders. But he hung out with others some thought he shouldn't spend time with, and he elevated those who had often been on the margins of society. In John 17 Jesus prays for his future followers; I would say that includes those of us trying to follow Jesus today. In his prayer, he prays that we would be "brought to complete unity." I have to conclude that Jesus didn't mean complete "sameness," since God intentionally created us all so different and unique. Jesus created us with a capacity for unity not uniformity.

Most churches and faith groups want to define who they are by what they believe. That seems like a clear way to identify yourself, but Jesus led his followers to be people who worked together in a common mission, not people with a common belief set on all things. The disciples and early Christians certainly had some differences of opinion, but they moved in the same general direction guided by a shared purpose. All churches are theologically and ideologically diverse because no two people are identical in their perspectives. But it's anxiety producing for faith communities and their leaders to admit this diversity when all that is holding them together is *supposed* intellectual agreement (more on this in chapter 17).

But like anything else that Jesus hopes for us, there are barriers to experiencing unity. I want to name some of these barriers and some responses that could be helpful as we experience the significantly different perspectives of those around us. One important note before we go on: I want to emphasize again the importance of healthy boundaries. Unity does not require enmeshment, being controlled by others, or sacrificing who you are for the sake of the group. If you find yourself in a relational situation that is unhealthy for you, the boundaries may need to be significant. Additionally, if you find yourself in an abusive situation in a relationship, family, or community, that is a completely different reality, and dissociating and getting help is a must! Final caveat: While I am encouraging you not to completely dissociate from someone who is different from you, there are times when finding a different faith community would be appropriate and finding others who can also be family to you when the differences with your relatives create a lack of support is beneficial.

Who Are My Mother and Brothers?

Jesus is giving a sermon to a group of people, and his mother and brothers show up outside the venue.[1] Someone comes to Jesus and lets him know that his family is outside waiting for him. His response is strange. He asks a question, as usual, "Who is my mother, and who are my brothers?" Then he points to his disciples and says, "Here are my mother and my brothers. For whoever does the will of my Father in heaven is my brother and sister and mother." There has been a lot of debate on what exactly Jesus was trying to say in this intriguing moment. My take is that there are some things that are so important to pursue that even your family has to wait and give you the space to do what you need to do. It seems like Jesus was also giving his "framily plan," expressing that sometimes your friends who you do life and mission with also need to be your family.

However, later in the story, Jesus absolutely shows his dedication to his mother and brothers. He wasn't disowning them; he was expressing the priorities that he needed to have. In our lives, the expansion we experience in our faith will no doubt impact those around us, especially those closest to us. It could be our parents or extended family, especially if we come from a family that is easily anxious if all members don't ascribe to faith in the often-narrow path they have come to deem as necessary for all. Others might realize that their spouse or closest friends are most affected by their questions and doubts. This is very common, and it is no doubt difficult for anyone to feel the stretching that happens in these relationships as you are experiencing yourself being stretched. In these scenarios, I think Jesus's example is helpful: Do everything you can to care for the well-being of your family and friends, but know that some of the spiritual discovery you need to do might make others uncomfortable. If it's important work to do, then you need to prioritize it. You may need to let others in who can come alongside you as family.

I encourage you yet again—especially with close family, friends, and especially your spouse—to resist the urge to sever ties. Choose healthy boundaries rather than estrangement. Choose courageous conversations rather than contentious arguments. Growth and expansion may cause a strain on your relationship, but they could also bring long-term growth for the other person and for your relationship as well. I have seen this happen many times where the spiritual renewal for one person has a ripple effect on those closest to them. It just may take time and openness on your part as well as trust. Their story never looks the same as yours, because everyone's journey is different. Here's a hard reality: even if that person never chooses to grow in their spiritual life, it's not possible to superficially hold yourself back from your own discovery in some sort of effort not to bypass them in some way. You can try, but it will nearly always end up in a dark place. It's not a race or a ladder in which you can be ahead or higher than others anyway. That's not a helpful frame for spirituality. Instead, have courage and keep going one step at a time. I love what Brené Brown says— "courage is contagious." Not everyone will catch it, but courage is worth it even if it's merely for you.

Whose Side Are You on Anyway?

A common barrier to finding unity in diversity is the fear of "getting it wrong." This fear is pervasive in Christianity and religion in general. I see this fear leading people to quickly pick a side rather than choosing to think through the various perspectives on an important issue or topic. The fear of getting it wrong can come from a desire to appear certain and confident and not come across as unsure. It can also lead to deep anxiety. For instance, I have heard many stories from people who suffer from what some call *salvation anxiety*—the fear that the wrong misstep will land them in hell.

Frankly, a God who threatens people with hell for one small misstep doesn't sound very much like the God of the Bible we see incarnated in the person of Jesus. In fact, that image of God sounds more like the other gods of the ancient Near East, the overarching culture during the time of the Bible. These gods were all different depending on the narrative, but what they had in common was a tendency to get angry easily, a lack of compassion, and a need to be appeased through certain specific behaviors. At best, these gods might require some sort of prayer or offering, at worst, the killing of children offered as a sacrifice.

Getting it right and picking a side cause us to elevate rightness to something we can and should achieve, and inadvertently communicate that getting it "wrong" is the worst possible outcome. It keeps humility and curiosity at bay and increases pride and arrogance. This need to pick the right side is intertwined with a troubling issue that is easy to see these days: dualistic or binary thinking, which divides concepts into two opposed or contrasted aspects without leaving room for other options. Classic dualistic thinking separates things between right and wrong, or good and evil. Dualistic thinking is easy to fall into, because it creates a shortcut for our brains. We naturally put things into categories, so having just two options to choose from makes it easy on us mentally. By comparing or understanding something in opposition to something else, we avoid the work of understanding it for what it actually is.

This binary thinking is a strong force and leads us to the inevitable conclusion that some Christians are the right kind of Christian and some are the wrong kind. In this view, there are really only two options—no room for the reality of the complexities of the life of faith. These simplistic divisions are all around us: conservative or liberal, traditional or progressive, Republican or Democrat. Dualism demands that we take sides and declare which camp we belong to. But Jesus never declared a camp. The religious leaders constantly tried to trap him, as I mentioned earlier. Was he a zealot who would lead a political uprising against Rome? Was he a new kind of Pharisee trying to hold people to the law? He couldn't be pegged. Jesus's story proves that resisting dualism can even get you killed. I know that isn't the most encouraging realization, but it shows how far Jesus would go to avoid the traps that dualism creates.

Dualism leaves no room for nuance. There are not only "two roads diverged in the yellow wood," as poet Robert Frost has unintentionally led us to believe. Dualism causes us to begin thinking that we must be either this or that. For instance, many would say that current American political rhetoric suggests that you can't care about babies in wombs as well as babies on the border of the United States being separated from their undocumented parents. At times, dualism seems to suggest that you have to agree with everything about someone's lifestyle in order to want them to have equal rights or to offer support. Dualism doesn't account for all the ways these concepts are interconnected because they are complex. The problem is that there is no space for gray in the black-and-white reality created by binary thinking. Because this way of thinking is so pervasive, it takes intentionality and effort to think with nuance, creativity, humility, and the goal of discovering deeper truth—rather than reaffirming the truth you already subscribe to.

Choosing this deeper way of thinking can be an important way we can show up to the relationships we have with those who think differently than us about our faith, politics, or other aspects of life. This depth of thought and ability to hold tension is the only way to have unity rather than uniformity. It's the only way we will experience the beauty of diversity and avoid the echo chamber caused by increased homogeneity. I've pressed in and stayed in relationships of difference, and I'm convinced it's worth the work and energy.

The Arrogance of Assumed Rightness

Some of the most rigid religious people I know are atheists who used to be fundamentalist Christians. Instead of leaving the rigid fundamentalism of Christianity for a more thoughtful approach to their faith, they are now fundamentalist atheists, rejecting anyone who believes that something other than science rules the universe as crazy and clearly in error. I see them as victims of dualistic thinking yet again.

Psychological certainty, which I have already claimed is a myth, leads to what theologian Greg Boyd calls "the arrogance of assumed rightness." This is a very slippery slope to hypocrisy and entitlement. People tend to believe they are right beyond any doubt, but that others need to be more willing to question their belief set. The willingness to embrace tension and nuance and to reject dualistic thinking is an opportunity to pursue intellectual and spiritual humility. The seemingly desperate need some people have to declare that they are right and others are wrong almost always stems from fear and insecurity. I've also observed that people don't like it when you tell them that you think they might be afraid and insecure. I know I don't want to be someone who succumbs to the arrogance of rightness, yet I, too, am guilty of the drive to prove I am right and others are wrong.

Humility is a beautiful quality, but spiritual elitism is not a good look on anyone. I have heard it come out of my own mouth, and it tastes bitter. At my worst moments, I've said and done things with the intention of making someone else feel dumb or ignorant. Even if people don't have all the information, making them feel less than is not the effect I want to have on others. It furthers the right-versus-wrong Christian mentality that boxes us into the binary yet again. Those who stay curious ask questions like, "could you tell me how you came to your conclusion?" rather than offer statements like, "if you just think through what you are saying, you will see that your belief is just not reasonable." If we ourselves have a fear of uncertainty or an unwillingness to pursue what might seem gray, we are part of the problem. If we think we are so enlightened that others are far beneath our spiritual vantage point and are not worth our time, we are fueling arrogance.

Humility is being open to the idea that anyone can teach us something valuable. It is accepting the fact that we aren't able to have a complete perspective because there are always multiple perspectives, often many that are valid. A humble person is reflective, taking into account the breadth and depth of the Christian tradition and how long people have been interpreting

Scripture and theology, and coming to a vast array of conclusions. Humility and courage look like the choice to stay present to other people and to stay open to their experience of the world. It's choosing to stay curious about them and what God is up to in the world through the diverse display of beings we call the human race.

It takes intentionality, but experimenting in this area can provide significant growth in those who give it a try. The following are some experiments to move from dualistic thinking to holding the tension in relationships with those different from you.

Either/Or Experiment

For this experiment, you will need to get a snack that is both salty and sweet (for example salted caramels, Chicago Mix popcorn, or salty and sweet Chex Mix). While eating the snack, follow this guide:

- Try to focus on the saltiness for at least a minute. Notice how your brain is drawn toward or away from the salty aspect of what you can taste.
- Next, focus on the sweetness of the snack for at least a minute. Notice how your brain is drawn toward or away from the sweet aspect of what you can taste.
- Is this snack salty? Is this snack sweet? Ponder the fact that the answer to both questions is Yes.

- Consider that though there are two very different tastes present in this one snack, separating them is a false binary. This snack is both salty and sweet.

- Continue eating the snack and do your best to consider other false binaries you may experience in your life. Examples to get you started would be that you may experience both peace and sadness, that there are experiences in life that are both tragic and beautiful, that someone can be both good and broken.

This experiment helps us grow in dialectical thinking, which is an ability that shows cognitive strength. It is the ability to synthesize what seems like two opposing alternatives. When we grow in this ability, we are able to move past a more basic and often lazy cognitive function of dualistic thinking.

Table Fellowship Dinner

Food is often called the great equalizer because it is something that everyone needs. This experiment gives the experience of learning from others around a table where everyone is taking the same action of offering nourishment to their bodies through the food.

- Invite a group of people who are different from you and from each other to dinner for a time of table fellowship.

- They could be different in age, race, culture, sexuality, political party, or religion.
- You may invite them to your home or to eat in a public location.
- If they offer to host, let them.
- Ask if everyone is willing to share some of their life story over the meal. Everyone is given the invitation to share at whatever level they feel comfortable.
- As each person shares their story, do your best to seek to understand rather than thinking about the differences in their story from your own or preparing your thoughts on how you will share your story.
- As you listen, when you hear something that seems contrary to your understanding of the world, for that moment choose to surrender and submit your ideas to the other. Notice in your heart how humility grows and arrogance subsides.
- After the meal, thank everyone for the gift of hearing their story and encourage each person to share something affirming about the person to their right.

Interview the Other

Consider an area in your life where it would be very clear that someone is in another category than you. For instance, someone in a different political party, someone with a different religious background, or someone who grew up primarily in a different country. Ask them if you can interview them about their perspective because you are doing an experiment in seeking to understand people who are different from you.

You may come up with your own list of questions based on the specific person you are interviewing. Here are some questions to get you started:

- What current-event headline has affected you the most lately and in what way?
- What would you say are the best aspects of your religion/culture/political party?
- What would you change about your religion/culture/political party if you could?
- What are some ways that you feel like you, or people like you, are misunderstood?
- What stereotypes do you believe others have about your religion/culture/political party, and what do you agree with and disagree with?

Do your best just to listen and to ask questions. Unless the person asks you a question, continue to respond with additional questions. Ask any follow-up questions that seem appropriate to your prepared questions. Two great follow-up questions are: Could you tell me more about that? Could you help me understand this better?

The Handbook for Life?

We live inside an unfinished story.
—Rachel Held Evans

Like most people in a new relationship, I became nervous when I was dating my husband, JD, and he told me he wanted to introduce me to his parents. But they made me feel right at home! Dinner had barely started when they began to tell me stories about JD—stories that they told all evening. Most of them were ridiculous and hilarious, and I shouldn't have been surprised. My husband still has a way of winding up in strange circumstances that turn into great stories. I heard about the time he fell off his bike, ended up with his head stuck in a chain-link fence, and had to be rescued with the Jaws of Life! And the missionary Sunday he had been selected to carry the flag from a country where one of the missionaries served. He had been warned that the flag must never touch the ground, so when he realized he forgot to wear a belt that day, he had no choice but to let his pants fall to the ground in front of the whole church.

At the time, I wasn't sure if they were trying to scare me off or warn me, but either way, I was loving every minute of it. I was falling hard for this guy, and the chance to hear about the thirty-two years of his life before he met me was so fun and intriguing. Of course, as our relationship has grown, I have also heard some of the hard stories from his life, the things that broke his heart or were difficult for his family. But all of these stories are precious to me because I love him and *he* is precious to me. The more I get to know him, the more these stories make sense and help me understand him even more deeply.

This is why God's story is given to us through Scripture— a library of books that we have bound together and call the Bible. When you love someone and are in a relationship with them, you want to know their story. You want to know all the stories of their life in order to make deeper meaning from your relationship with them. This is exactly how I now experience the Bible and my relationship with God. The more I experience God in my life, the more interesting the Bible is to me.

The more I read and learn about the Bible, the deeper I experience God. But it wasn't always this way for me. It has taken me a long time to be confident that the Bible helps me deepen my faith rather than causes it to unravel.

Wrestling with Your Scriptures

Even now, though I approach the Bible with far less trepidation than I once did, I still find myself wrestling with Scripture and what it means for us today. I think I will wrestle with the Bible for the rest of my life. Thus, I join a long line of people trying to understand these ancient words and finding that it's not a simple task.

If you walked into any Jewish Synagogue today, you would find a Torah scroll containing the Jewish Scriptures written in ancient Hebrew. The Torah is the first five books of what Christians refer to as the Old Testament. Every Torah scroll is made with the utmost care and precision, following the law of Moses (which is itself a part of the Torah).

Every scroll is made out of parchment (a paper made from animal skin) and each page is sewn together with threads made from the sinew (fibrous tissue that connects muscle to the bone) of a kosher animal thigh.[1] This is done intentionally to remind the Jewish people of the story of one of their forefathers, Jacob, who wrestled with an angel. The story is usually seen as representing wrestling with God. The angel touches Jacob's hip and throws it out of its socket. Before the exchange is over, Jacob is given a new name, Israel, which means "one who wrestles with God." The Jewish people are later called *the people of Israel* or *the Israelites*. Living up to their name, they continue to sew thigh sinew into their scrolls because they expect to wrestle with Scripture every time they read it.[2]

The Bible and Its Reliability

One of the first things to notice about the Bible is that it's not a chapter book but rather a library of books. Each of these books falls into a different genre, or even multiple genres, and genre is one important way to determine the meaning of a piece of writing. The genres include narrative, law, poetry, prophecy, and apocalyptic books. You'll notice that "handbook for life" or "science textbook" or "magic answer book" are not included on that list, even though so many people act and talk like these are the *only* genres in the Bible!

The Bible is not a handbook that you can apply to twenty-first-century life. This doesn't mean that it isn't relevant to twenty-first-century life. It just means that you shouldn't try to make it into something it isn't. Try this exercise: look to see whether you have a handbook lying around at home (the instruction manual that came with your new Instant Pot, the owner's manual to your car, etc.). I have the handbook to my Mazda sitting next to my Bible right now so I can make a comparison. As I page through each thick book, I see that they could not be more different. I can read my Mazda handbook transactionally. By reading a sentence or paragraph plainly, I can easily find the answers to my questions. If the check-engine light is on in my car's dashboard, I simply turn to page 27 and read some bullet points that help me get to the bottom of the problem. The Bible just doesn't work this way—it's not transactional. If you have warning lights going off in your life, the Bible can be extremely helpful. But it won't be as simple as reading some bullet points on page 27. Sure, it might be nice if it was designed that way. But it wasn't.

Some people point to the Bible's lack of straightforward answers as evidence that the Bible isn't reliable. To that, all I can say is that the Bible is not reliable for doing things it was never intended for.

Is the Bible reliable as a magic answer book? No. Sorry.

Is it a science or history textbook designed for readers to scrutinize with the precision of modern scientific or historical methods? I don't think so.

However, is it a reliable collection of various books and genres that give us a deep and complex look at the story of God? Yes. This is exactly what it is intended for!

Is it a reliable tool for shaping our understanding of how humans have responded to God throughout the history of humanity? I think so!

Is Scripture reliable as a greater narrative that we can see our own stories within? Absolutely.

Is the Bible reliable as a library we can use to shape our lives that can be transformational (rather than transactional)? Yes!

The Bible is reliable, but only to do what it was intended to do. We will have to wrestle and struggle through the complexity of an ancient book that wasn't written *to* us but is absolutely relevant *for* us.

The Tapestry of Stories

If you're reading this book, you might have grown up in a home that valued the Bible and heard it talked about like it *was* a handbook to life. So the perspective I'm offering can sometimes feel disorienting. It can feel like a thread was pulled, and your understanding of the Bible is unraveling before your eyes!

For thousands of years, various cultures around the world—from the Greeks to the Japanese—have used tapestries to tell stories. Historically, weaving a tapestry was nearly always a community effort. Many were so large that it would take multiple people multiple years to complete. Intricate images woven with the loom would represent multiple genres and concepts from narrative to ancient poetry, all in a single tapestry. It could easily take days or weeks to fully grasp all that was depicted. Yet, one single tapestry could never represent fully the stories it was trying to depict.

We can think about the Bible like a tapestry. A community of people led by God came together to interweave stories, poems, genealogies, and other genres to try to represent a huge story. The story is so grand and epic that it would never fit into a single book, or even a sixty-six-book library. If you carefully study each thread, over time you will get a pretty good idea of the story. But there is so much woven into this story that it would take more than a lifetime to grasp it fully. The good news is we have our whole lives to give it a shot. Scripture is a "living word,"[3] as the writers of Hebrews call it, so none of us can expect to master it. In fact, Scripture has infinitely deeper meanings as a person, or a community, continues to engage with it.

Here is the thing about a tapestry: even if you realize that some of it is beginning to unravel, it is not in danger of unraveling to the point of destruction. It would take a lot more than pulling a thread or two to dismantle the warp (the vertical thread that provides structure) from the horizontally woven threads that tell the story. I like to think of proper exegesis (study of what the text meant in its original context) and intentional hermeneutics (study of the meaning and relevance of the text to today) as the warp of the tapestry of Scripture. The warp keeps the horizontal thread in place and helps the depiction of the story to be visible and clear.

Weaving a Story of Healing

I live in the urban center of Minneapolis, and while there are many wonderful things to say about my city, our community also struggles with destructive things like gang violence. Many young lives have been lost, and it has devastated communities again and again. A quaint house on the corner of a rough street has been set aside as a retreat for those who need a space of refuge and healing. A group of Catholic nuns oversee this home, named the St. Jane House. In the house is a beautiful Japanese loom that those who retreat there are able to use to make a tapestry. A spiritual guide helps the sojourner weave a tapestry of healing.

A woman named Mary Johnson lost her son to gang violence in that neighborhood, but she later befriended Oshea, the man who shot her son. Today, Oshea and Mary call each other "spiritual mother and son." This beautiful story of healing has birthed a movement called From Death to Life, led by Mary. She brings mothers who have lost their sons and daughters to violence and drugs to the St. Jane House to weave their own healing tapestry. These mothers bring with them strips of cloth from their child's clothing or fabric that represents their child's favorite color or sports team. They gather with other women telling stories of the children they have lost while weaving the thread onto the warp. These children's lives may have ended, but they are still a part of their mothers' stories, and healing is needed in order to move into the future after such a tragedy. The mothers' lives continue, as they are still in the messy middle of their own stories.

The Bible as a story is not complete. We have the beginning (creation), a crisis (fall), some of the messy middle (redemption), and then a vision of how the story will end (restoration). God created a world that was good, brokenness entered the world, and from that moment on, God began a work of redemption— God's mission to redeem the world that God loves. The end of the story is termed *restoration* because it looks forward to a day when the world is fully redeemed, and all that has gone wrong is made right. One of the things I cling to the most in life is that even though John's vision written down in Revelation is cryptic and confusing, it shows us that brokenness is not the end of the story!

If you're following me so far, you might realize that most of the entire tapestry of Scripture is the redemption portion of the story (from Genesis 8 to Jude). Sometimes, when you plop down in the middle of 2 Kings, it doesn't seem like you are in the messy middle of redemption. But if you zoom back out, you'll see that you were reading right in the middle of the mess being redeemed!

Here we are in the twenty-first century, still living in the messy middle of the story. The tapestry of God's story isn't complete; it's in process. We see the beginning, the crisis, and a portion of the messy middle, but we are still living right smack in the messy middle ourselves. I don't know about you, but I have experiences nearly every day that remind me we're still in the messy middle. We are all a mess! But God has been on the redemptive trajectory for many pages—or threads if you will. Your story matters inside this greater story and so does mine. The fabric of our lives can be woven into the story as part of the larger tapestry.

If you were to take some time to observe your own story as part of the tapestry, my guess is that you will find that it brings healing—just like it does for those mothers at the St. Jane House. When you see the big story as God's, with our lives woven in as supporting characters, it pries our hearts from ego-centrism, helps us see the bigger picture of God's movement around us, and invites us to be a part of this messy middle of redemption! We get to play a part in the story, making wrong things right, joining in with God as we were designed to do.

In the last few hours of Jesus's life, he shared his heart with the women and men who had spent nearly every waking moment of the last three years with him. In my Bible, the words of Jesus are in red letters, and nearly all of John 14–17 is in red. I suppose most of us would be pouring out our hearts if we knew we only had a few hours left with our loved ones. Near the end of Jesus's words to his friends, he says, "I have much more to say to you, more than you can now bear. But when he, the Spirit of truth, comes he will guide you into all the truth."[4] Jesus has already said so much, but yet has so much more to say. His words remind me that there is only so much any of us can take in at one time, especially during trying times. This was certainly one of those times for these disciples.

Most of us would love to have a full understanding of the Bible and not have to wrestle like Jacob with the angel. We'd prefer not to have our hip knocked out of its socket, thank you very much! But that opportunity is not given to us. And beware of anyone who suggests that it is. Phrases like "the Bible clearly says" are dangerous. Each of us comes to the Bible with only our own cultural, generational, and socioeconomic perspective on a text written thousands of years ago. Too often, we arrogantly believe that our perspective is the only right one. The Bible can lead you to some to clarity, but to do so takes a lot of intentionality, effort, exegesis, hermeneutics, and, as Jesus said, guidance by the Holy Spirit.

I hope that you choose to stay curious about the Bible, recognizing that none of us will ever fully master one of the most complex and interesting texts that exist. Don't run from the questions that bubble up in you about the Bible; dig into them! Be sure to vet the external sources that you pursue to help inform you, but let your intrigue and questions guide you. You just may find that Jesus was right, and the Holy Spirit meets you within them. God will lead you to answers at a rate that you can bear. You will come to new conclusions, but no doubt you will be led to deeper questions as well. So it's best to get used to them!

There are three practices I want to offer you that give you the opportunity to approach the Bible in very different ways. These are great experiments to help you discover and wonder how your relationship with the Bible might shift, grow, change, or even begin!

Here are some experiments that offer a different approach to the Bible.

Prayer of Imagination

The idea behind this experiment is to imagine yourself in the midst of some of the most compelling stories about Jesus. This experiment is best done with a different passage every day for a week. For example, you might try these: Matthew 9:18–26, Matthew 14:22–33, Mark 2:1–12, Luke 7:1–10, Luke 7:36–50, John 4:7–26, and John 8:1–11.

- Choose a translation that seems clear to you. The Message version by Eugene Peterson is good for this experiment because while it is not as scholastically accurate, it has powerful imagery and accessible language.
- Open the passage and read it slowly, imagining yourself as a bystander in the scene.
- Next, read it again, but this time, imagine you are one of the characters in the story.
- Read it a third time, and try to imagine what the scene would look like from Jesus's eyes.
- Consider the character traits of Jesus in this story and how they reflect the character of the Trinitarian God.

Find a conversation partner and talk through what you discovered in this experiment.

The Bible Project

There is a website, TheBibleProject.com, where some scholars have made artistic videos that explain the major themes of the

Bible. The videos and other resources are free to use. There are multiple themes told through five-minute videos.

- For this experiment, take two weeks to watch all the videos.
- Wonder about the experience you have had with the Bible in your life up to this point. How does it compare to these stories? What is familiar? What is bringing new perspective?
- As you watch the videos, consider the reality of God as the main character of the overarching story.
- In each video, what is God as the main character trying to accomplish?

Find a conversation partner and talk through what you discovered in this experiment.

Metanarrative Mind Map

The overarching story we see through the Bible is referred to as the *metanarrative*. For this experiment, compare and contrast the following two-sentence descriptions of the metanarrative.

Narrative 1: The Bible is about human sin management and hell avoidance.

Narrative 2: The Bible is about God restoring all things and inviting humans to join in.

On a sheet of paper, draw a line vertically down the middle. On the left side, name everything you can think of that leads to narrative 1. On the right side, name everything you can think of that leads to narrative 2. (For example: life experiences, specific Bible stories, cultural realities.)

On an additional sheet of paper, create two columns again, but this time write on the left side what is produced from narrative 1 in people's lives and in the world. On the right side, do the same for narrative 2. (For example: ideologies, perspectives on the world, actions people take, religious practices, etc.)

Compare and contrast your lists. What do you notice? Are there significant differences between the two lists? Which of the two narratives has been most pervasive in your life? Is there a third or fourth narrative you would submit? Were certain columns on either sheet easier or harder for you to fill out? Why might that be?

Find a conversation partner and talk through what you discovered in this experiment.

The Big C

Maybe God has given some people belief like a pier, to stand on (and God has given those people's steadiness to the church, to me, as a reminder, as an aid), and maybe God has given others something else: maybe God has given to some this humming sense that we know nothing, this belief and disbelief a hundred times an hour, this training in nimbleness (and maybe that is a gift to the church, too).
—Lauren Winner

I grew up in a ministry family. What I mean by this is that my parents were in full-time vocational Christian ministry while I was growing up. While many people grow up in this environment, no two experiences are the same. Even my brother, who is only two years younger than me, had a distinctly different experience than I did. There is always some pressure for kids of pastors and missionaries to go into the family business, just like there would be for a family with nurses, teachers, or lawyers. However, I didn't feel particularly pressured to take on vocational ministry as a profession. I went to college with my sights set on many different career paths, none of which were ministry related.

This all changed when I began to think more critically about my experience growing up so involved in the church. In the past twenty years or so, much of the seedy underbelly of the church has been revealed to the masses. I, for one, am glad that some of what was hidden in the darkness has come to the light. I think that these scandals being exposed can bring freedom to those who were victims of crimes like clergy sexual abuse and assault. Not to mention the situations of financial deception and spiritual manipulation—the list could go on. Individual churches have issues, but so does the "Big C" Church, as I call it. By the "Big C" Church, I mean the entire movement of people mobilized to follow Jesus, regardless of their worship service attendance, not merely one specific local church.

In my early twenties, as I was starting to grow and expand as a person, I began to deconstruct all that I had seen in the church and in the ministries my family was involved in. This was a painful but very important process for me. Finally, I got to a place where I could respect what my parents had been trying to do and celebrate the wonderful aspects of their efforts. However, I could also see the blind spots and missteps of the organizations and local churches they had helped to lead. It was in the middle of that deconstruction that I began to think that vocational ministry was part of who I was created to be, to lead the church in some way.

I was in a difficult spot—feeling drawn to lead the same movement that I was currently so disappointed and disillusioned with. I had grown up thinking the church was *mostly* perfect. I had believed the excuse that the imperfections, some of which I had witnessed firsthand, were just rare occurrences. But I realized that the brokenness of the church was the norm, because the brokenness of humans is the norm. Gone was my blind optimism and in its place came realism that bordered on pessimism. So for a while I fought this sense that I was supposed to take up the family business. Whenever I try to avoid something that I know deep down in my soul I am supposed to pursue, I feel miserable. Not moving toward what you are wired for will result in frustration, and that was certainly true for me.

Everything finally came to a boiling point, and I had to face it head on. I climbed a hill that gave me a vantage point on Minneapolis and had a wrestling match with God. I tried to reconcile in my heart and mind how I could feel drawn to lead something that I had so many questions, concerns, and fears about. I could only see two options ahead of me. I could completely reject the church and all that I had seen it do to hurt people and cause pain and suffering. Or, I could commit to this sense that I was supposed to be a leader in the church and thus commit to being part of the change that needed to happen. I came down from that hill with very few of my questions answered but with a sense of conviction and resolution that has never left me. I committed to following this sense of calling that I could no longer ignore, but only because I believed redemption was possible in the church, and I wanted to be a part of the change that needed to happen.

Of course, I was experiencing a utopian hope that eventually led to a utopian slope when I realized how hard change truly is and how much going against the grain would cost me personally. I realized, too, that I was a broken person, so there was a good chance I'd hurt some people along the way, because that's what broken humans do. Even when they try their best not to.

The Vehicle for God's Mission

In order to be a part of the change that I wished to see in the church, I had to make a number of paradigm shifts, but the most important of them all was the shift I made from seeing the church as the end goal of Christianity to seeing it as a *means* to the end goal of Christianity. Several of my mentors, like Dr.

Craig Van Gelder and Dr. Dwight Zscheile, have said something similar to this: "The church is not God's mission, rather it is a vehicle for God's mission." God could have accomplished the redemption-mission part of the messy middle of this story without our help, but God designed the whole mission to be dependent on human participation.[1]

So if the church is a vehicle for God's mission, then imagine with me each local church as an actual vehicle. Some are minivans, some are station wagons, others are buses or Volkswagen Beetles. Perhaps a vehicle type immediately comes to mind to represent your current or former church. I think mine would be a fifteen-passenger van with no air conditioning (we actually have no air conditioning in the school where we worship, so it fits). Some people are in their particular vehicle because that is the one they have always been in. Some of my Lutheran friends, for instance, call themselves "cradle to grave Lutherans." I have also heard some Baptists say they are "ride or die Baptists." It reminds me of people whose families only drove Fords or Subarus while they were growing up, so they can't imagine driving anything else when they purchase their own car. There is nothing wrong with this kind of loyalty, as long as we remember that there's no way to judge another vehicle unless you try it out first. The Ford families should be cautious to criticize the Subaru families if they've never even taken an Outback for a spin!

Some people are not at all committed to a certain brand, make, or model of vehicle. Instead, they are interested in comparing the experience of driving one vehicle or another. Some, if they are honest, prefer a shiny new vehicle. They get in and notice if the seats are comfortable, if the air conditioning is at the right temperature, and then, most importantly, what radio station is on and if they like it. If it is too loud, quiet, slow, fast, cheesy, old, new, they may get out and try a different vehicle.

Others have a similar approach but are perhaps asking deeper questions like, What is the reliability of this vehicle? How is it rated for safety? Do the seat belts and airbags work? They have been hurt by the lack of safety in the past or are unsure if they want to go anywhere in a vehicle that might break down and leave them stranded. All valid questions! Perhaps even more important are the other people sitting next to you in the car. What are they like? Do they agree with the words and songs playing in this car? Do they see the world the same way I do?

At the end of the day, most people pick their church based on belief system and amenities. They're looking for a group of people who believe the same things they do and an atmosphere that feels comfortable. This naturally leads churches to aim for the right mix of beliefs and amenities so that their car is full, maybe even in need of an upgrade soon because so many people want a chance to sit in this awesome vehicle with people who agree with them!

One important question seems to be missing in all of this: Where is this vehicle going?

Where is it taking you? Where is it taking us as a family or a community? Is it dropping us off anywhere different than where it started to when we first got in? My church growing up had a lot of wonderful qualities, though I would have preferred we change the proverbial radio station from the oldies to current hits. But the glaring gap I see when I look back was that it seemed like people got into the church van every Sunday morning, and we drove around the block just to be let out right where were started in the first place.

This is what I mean when I say that the church has become the end goal rather than a vehicle that takes us somewhere, a vehicle by which God's redemption mission is executed in the world. My hope for my fifteen-passenger van is that we are honest about the fact that the air conditioning is broken. I hope the seat belts work and the oil gets changed so that we are as safe as we can be. Safety is important because the journey we are on may not be completely safe. Jesus is in the driver's seat, after all! The stories about what happens when that guy is driving aren't always safe, but they're always good. My goal as a leader is to tune the radio to a station that helps people know the driver of the van better so that they trust where he is taking them. My hope is that people would get out of the van every week somewhere new—perhaps a place where they have courage to encounter relationships with people different from them or can trust that the storm raging outside the van is something they are not alone in facing. I hope that they will get out at a new spot where they'll see opportunities to join actively in mercy and justice, that their new vantage point will help them see their part in the mission of redemption to the world that God loves.

Along the ride, I do hope they'll ask questions about what they believe, and that they will be okay with people in seats next to them coming to different conclusions. They will realize that people with different perspectives help them grow in understanding of others and of God. Ultimately, they will see that what bonds this little local church together isn't that we all love the radio station, the upholstery, the paint job on the outside, or the snacks. That what brings us together isn't even that we all believe the same thing about God, the Bible, and Jesus. But rather, I hope they will see, even when they encounter differences and difficulties, that this van is being driven by Jesus. Not in circles but toward a mission that will only be accomplished if everyone joins in!

Your Story Is Welcome Here

When trying to decide if you want to stay in your current church vehicle—or whether you want to try rejoining a church or joining one for the first time—you will undoubtably have a lot of questions. It makes sense that you'd want your seat in the vehicle to feel right. The most important questions to ask are these:

- Who is driving this vehicle? Is it actually a human when it should be Jesus?
- Do the leaders riding shotgun desire to trust Jesus's leadership and navigation?
- Where does it seem like this vehicle is going?
- Does the vehicle let you out at a new stop on the journey or right back where you started when you got in?
- Do the seat belts work and are people encouraged to use them so that everyone can be spiritually and emotionally safe?
- Are the people in the car open to wrestling through questions or does it seem like we all have to think the same thing in order to have a seat?
- Does everyone in the vehicle want to be challenged by the rough terrain the vehicle will face?

The final question is a really important one.

- Is my story welcome here and is everyone in the van encouraged to listen to others' stories?

Your story is a part of God's story, so we aren't complete if everyone's story isn't welcome. We can be people who disagree with each other, but you can't disagree with someone's story. You may disagree with the conclusions they have formed from their story, but that would require listening to and welcoming their story in the first place.

As a pastor, I want you to know that your story is needed in the church—even if your story has some very dark chapters or some pages about anger, depression, addiction, or doubt. In fact, others riding in the vehicle with you will benefit from hearing your honest story—they'll likely have some shared experiences. The church needs those who have relentless curiosity and unending questions. Your story of joy and celebration is needed, too, so that everyone in the vehicle can be encouraged. They will need that encouragement when they get out of the vehicle and find themselves in a new place. Your story being welcome doesn't mean that there isn't room for change or growth. Healthy organisms and healthy humans are always growing, but no one should be expected to grow if they cannot be heard and received by others.

In addition to questions for the church, it is important to ask yourself some questions:

- How do you see your story fitting into God's larger story?
- How do you see your purpose in joining in the redemption mission of this messy middle of the story?
- Whose story will yours need to intertwine with in order to have the support you need?
- How will you find others who see their story as important to the overarching story so that you can be better and stronger together as you join in the redemption mission?

- How can you overcome some of what makes community uncomfortable in order to stay present and grow?

These are all questions about what it means to be a part of not merely the local church but the "Big C" Church. So consider wherever you are at in your process of understanding your spot in God's church valid. But what is your next step?

Here are some experiments you can try to move forward in answering these questions about the "Big C" Church as well as your local church. Find your own pace. I encourage you to push yourself past your comfort zone, but don't obliterate it!

Cathedral or Sanctuary Discovery

Visit a cathedral or sanctuary—the more ornate and artistic the better. If you are unable to visit a cathedral in your area, search "3D Cathedral" online and use one of those options. However, if you are able to visit in person, this will be ideal.

- When you arrive at the cathedral, find a place to sit where you can see as much of the interior design of the space.
- Begin by inviting God's presence to be with you as you wonder about the creation of this space.
- Imagine what the original designers and builders of this building were trying to create by investing in this space. What was their original intent?
- What do you think they were trying to express to God?

- What might they have been trying to express to the world?
- What do you notice about yourself in this space? What emotions does it bring up? Do you feel able to focus or do you find this space distracting?
- Ponder what the phrase *a holy space* means to you given your life experiences.
- Ask Jesus to give you his eyes for this space and for the people who come to worship him in it.
- If appropriate, walk around the space noticing what is on the walls, the ceiling, the altar, and so on.

Find a conversation partner and talk through what you discovered in this experiment.

Spiritual Practice of Fellowship

Experiencing the "Big C" Church is not confined to worship services or church buildings. This experiment will involve inviting at least three Jesus followers to join you. In fact, if you could get closer to ten or twelve, that would be even better! They may be regularly attending a local church, or they may not. The only requirement is that they are people who would say they are trying to follow Jesus, even if they have doubts and questions.

- Once you invite your guests, compare schedules.

- Over a three-month period, find a time that you can all have a meal together at least once a month.
- When you gather for dinner, have a potluck rather than any one person or family having to provide the meal.
- While eating, take time to do some intentional story-telling. Here are some questions to guide your time; feel free to come up with your own:
  - What has faith and spirituality looked like from your childhood until today?
  - What are some of the biggest questions you have about faith and Christianity?
  - What has been helpful, if anything, to move through the questions and doubts you've faced?
  - If you can, name ways you've seen God move in your life in the last year/month/week?
- Do everything you can to avoid offering advice or suggestions to others. Rather, ask intentional follow-up questions in order to go deeper. After each person shares, thank them and move to the next person.
- Before the meal is over, have each person or family share one way that the others could serve them. It's not that you need help; rather intentionally choose to let others serve you. For instance, raking your yard together or bringing meals during a busy week. Spread out the serving over the three months, and be sure everyone is served at least once.

- There is a good chance in a group like this over three months someone will go through an ordeal in their life. Encourage the group to surround those going through the situation with prayer and support.
- After the third meal, have everyone talk through the experiment and what you learned from trying this out together.

Diverse Worship Experience

Visit a church or worship service of a different ethnic background than your own. It is amazing how this can help us open our perspective on the purpose of the church. A myopic view of the church in the world holds us back from seeing the breadth and depth of the diversity of the universal church. Perpetual doubt and cynicism can be fueled on ethnocentrism and homogeneity.

- Look online for churches that you are able to visit.
- Find a friend who might be willing to join you.
- Come early but be prepared for this group of people to view time differently than your cultural context.
- Consider that the service may be shorter or longer than you may be used to and plan accordingly so you don't need to leave early.
- If you are invited to a social hour after worship, do your best to join in even though it might be intimidating.

- While you are with this worship community ask yourself the following questions:
  - What feels familiar to you?
  - What feels different and new to you?
  - What do you notice about how this group talks about God?
  - What do you notice about how this community worships (music, readings, liturgy, etc.)?
  - What do you notice about how this community engages with the Bible?
  - What about this experience do you want to take with you to continue to ponder and wonder about?

Talk with the friend who came with you or find a conversation partner and talk through what you discovered in this experiment.

Slacktivism and Other Dangers

*Never forget that justice is what
love looks like in public.*
—Cornel West

Crises of faith are sparked for many reasons. My friend Stefan's was spurred on by a watershed moment. He was driving through his neighborhood and realized a glaring discrepancy between his own life and his growing understanding of Jesus. It dawned on him that he didn't have any personal relationships with people who were considered poor or on the margins. As he drove through the streets, he could see people in need on his right and on his left. But he didn't know them by name, and he certainly couldn't have called any of them his friends.

In his walk of faith, Stefan focused on the person of Jesus—paying attention to how Jesus lived his life on earth, seeking a relationship with Jesus, and attempting to follow his example. Stefan didn't see following Jesus as a list of rights and wrongs. Rather, he constantly tried to join in what Jesus was still doing in the world around him. He realized that day that to follow Jesus, he was going to have to take to the streets. Jesus ministered in the streets and in the homes of those on the margins—spending time with the "prostitutes, sinners and tax collectors (traitors)." Jesus disregarded the holier-than-thou approach of his accusers and showed a new way of crossing societal boundaries, motivated by love.

Stefan started by visiting the parts of his neighborhood where those on the margins often spent time. He went to them, with no illusion that they would come to him. Most of us approach those in poverty from a place of privilege, but it is important to recognize that those on the margins have important gifts to bring us as well—for Stefan, the poor in his community displayed a proximity to Jesus he was searching for.

Over time, Stefan developed some important relationships with the people he connected with on the streets. He now calls this his "Nicodemus experience." I've mentioned Nicodemus, whose story is told in John 3. He was a Jewish religious leader who was drawn to Jesus and had to find a way to get to him.

So he waited until nightfall when the crowds had left, and he approached Jesus to ask the questions burning in his heart. Jesus didn't answer all of Nic's questions. Instead, Nicodemus left with deeper questions than he came with in the first place. Typical for Jesus, the question man, not the answer man.

When Stefan discovered Jesus on the streets through his new friends, it changed the trajectory of his life. It's been nearly two decades since his "Nicodemus experience," and he has had more than his fair share of faith questions—but he hasn't had another faith crisis. I think I know why. It is what's possible when we recognize that complete certainty is not necessary for strong conviction.

Online Activism and Its False Sense of Action

Saturday Night Live aired a sketch a few years ago that has come to be known as "Thank You, Scott." Scott is depicted as a man who spends most of his time at home watching TV and scrolling the internet. Every few seconds, Scott becomes agitated by something he sees on the news or web, so he takes to Facebook. He posts his outrage with the perfect hashtag to show what side of the activism he is on. The other actors from SNL sing a sarcastic song about how thankful they are to Scott. *People* called the song the "anthem for those who are fighting social injustices with their keyboards."[1] Scott is shown reading an article about the refugee crisis and posting about it in his newsfeed as the actors sing, "You solved the problem, Scott! You brought the struggle to an end, Scott, by sharing that article with eighty-four Facebook friends!"

Slacktivist is the label used for the people parodied by the "Thank You, Scott" sketch. The deepest problem with slacktivism is that it gives a false sense of action. People who share articles online feel as though they have taken action against injustice, when they really haven't. I think of taking action and participating in justice as soul food. It brings a sense of fullness to your life and is more than just temporary. Jesus promises this kind of soul nourishment in John 10:10 when he offers full life. We don't want our lives to be busy, but we should desire for them to be full. Full of purpose, full of meaning, even a full schedule—not just busyness.

Slacktivism is like eating a candy bar for lunch. You feel full for a little while, but soon you are left feeling hungry again. It doesn't lead to true fullness—or health for that matter! The temptation to give in to slacktivism is very real and can come in many forms, not just online. For example: buying merchandise from social entrepreneurs, wearing shirts that support marginalized groups without having friendships with those the shirt represents, or signing up for the email newsletter from an NGO that you admire. There is nothing wrong with any of these actions! They are only a danger to you when you believe that they are a substitute for actually working for change out in the world. The rubber meets the road when you start to hold back on luxuries in life in order to financially support the NGO or ministry that is caring for those in need. It's true activism when you send those Christmas gifts to kids in need once a year but *also* decide to regularly mentor a child who needs a friend right in your city.

A pervasive idea—that mercy is something that only organizations, governments, and churches are responsible for and not also individuals and families—has infected the church in America. A recent Barna poll found that only 17 percent of American Christians believe that mercy is also a personal responsibility.[2] But I'm encouraged to see that mercy is still a big motivator for Jesus followers; 63 percent say that "mercy is something that often influences the words or actions that I choose."[3]

Many of us have a desire to participate, but we are held back from personal activism and action because it's hard and uncomfortable, and we tend to run away from both difficulty and discomfort. But even if we can overcome these obstacles, there is something else that can get in the way of action: the idea that we need certainty in order to have conviction. If you've made it this far into the book, you know that certainty is a myth that cannot be found no matter how hard we try. Of course, we can have faith that what we believe is true, but we can't be 100 percent certain. When we think we are 100 percent certain, we may be worshipping certainty rather than an infinite God.

It's absolutely possible to have conviction without having certainty. In fact, following your conviction can actually help you move through the wilderness and break through the walls.

Acting on conviction is the kind of action that nourishes your soul, giving you the strength to keep moving forward. When you have convictions that God is calling you to act, step toward those convictions—not just by liking Facebook groups but by getting involved with your passion area in a tangible way on the ground. There have been so many times that I have followed the clickbait and felt like I had made a huge impact. "Thank You, Scott" could have easily been "Thank You, Steph!" But recently, I have had my own Nicodemus moment where I have stepped toward Jesus in a more direct way when something has broken my heart.

Bearing Witness

In the last few years, the worldwide refugee crisis has weighed heavily on me. Some people have been in exile for as long as I have been alive.[4] I have felt convicted to participate in some way with the restoration of this crisis and started with a time of learning—reading articles and books and watching documentaries. That is a good place to start because ignorance can lead to harm—both for yourself and others. Next, I realized that there are people in my own community who have been refugees. Minneapolis has a high population of resettled refugees from all around the world. I got to know some of these folks personally and have been able to hear their stories firsthand.

Next, I chose to financially support refugee resettlement organizations as well as financially sponsor a child who lives in a crisis-ravaged part of the world. Then, I encouraged and coached a group from my faith community who felt called to sponsor a family who was being resettled in Minneapolis. Their main goal was to offer hospitality and relationship to the family, who were coming to the United States for the first time.

None of this was easy; I am self-centered by nature (as are we all). It's so difficult to be intentional about hearing stories that make me uncomfortable. It's tempting to want to scale back the financial support when we have a hard month with unexpected expenses. I am sharing this example with you because I want you to know that I also wrestle with the temptation toward slacktivism. These steps haven't been easy, but they have brought a fuller life!

My husband and I have been trying to take these steps together, and it has brought us closer as well. Our growing passion led us to take a humanitarian trip to visit Bidibidi Refugee Settlement, currently the second-largest refugee settlement in the world. Bidibidi is in Uganda, on the border of South Sudan. The experience was life changing to say the least. It was expensive, and we know that the money could have gone to ongoing water projects and other needs in that region. However, we traveled with a group of others who, like us, have experience in marketing and storytelling. Our trip gave us the opportunity to tell the story of the work being done in that region and is leading to more awareness of the refugee crisis. The marketing work we have been able to do is increasing overall funding for this important work. We decided to go because we have a conviction that there are just some things that we need to *bear witness* to because they will shape our lives, and we will never be the same. This trip has been so significant that it has changed the stories we tell and will continue to shape the future actions we take.

Of course, we—and you—don't have to go across the world to bear witness to the convictions on our hearts. We've spent the night in homeless shelters, walked the streets and talked to women caught in sex-work, spent time with dancers at strip clubs and asked them about their dreams, mentored kids who only have a 50 percent chance of graduating high school, and welcomed refugees to our city with open arms—all within a five-mile radius of our house. At the end of the day, it's not because we're so great and have so much to offer (we aren't, and we don't). Every single one of those encounters has offered more to me than I was able to offer to the other person. It's been life changing every time. What are the convictions on your heart? If you haven't taken action on those convictions, what is holding you back?

You don't have to know it all or have it all figured out to take action right where you are. Set down the phone and realize this: the statistical chance that someone is going to change their mind from your emotionally charged Facebook post is slim to none. Taking action will do so much more for your soul—giving you the fuel you need to stay curious in your life.

Stefan had tons of questions as he developed deep relationships with those on the margins. Each new relationship just sparked more questions! But in the midst of it all, he became convinced that one-on-one relationships with people different from you can lead to life change for both parties. So he began to work to connect urban youth with one-on-one mentors— someone who needed a relationship with a resilient student that became their little brother or sister over time. From there, a nonprofit was birthed called One2One,[5] whose goal is to see the students (and mentors!) grow. The students report if they have grown in their relationships and motivation in school, but they also report if they have seen *their mentor grow* in patience and ability to listen before giving advice.

There is no need to take a trip or start a nonprofit to move from slacktivism to action. Here are some experiments that others have tried that have opened up their hearts and gotten them involved even when they had questions and uncertainties.

Neighborhood Resonate Walk

This experiment is designed to help you see deeper into the world around you in your everyday spaces.

- Take fifteen minutes and walk from your home or workplace around the neighborhood.
- Using a smart phone or camera, take photos of what resonates with you—anything that seems to draw your attention.
- Then, as you walk, pray and ask God if there is anything God wants to say to you.

- When you arrive back at your original location, look back over your photos and wonder why it was the images you took resonated with you.
- Ask again for God to reveal anything God might want to say to you.
- Here is an example from someone who tried this experiment:

I walked around my neighborhood and took a few photos of what resonated with me. The one that stuck out to me at the end is of a stone Jesus near my house. I didn't think that was going to be my photo I would choose at first, but then I got closer and saw that Jesus didn't have thumbs! Someone had broken them off! As I was walking, I felt like God asked me to think about what that might represent. As I walked and prayed, I began to think about how opposable thumbs are what gives you the ability to grasp things and how useless our hands would be without them. I thought about the church as the body of Christ and what causes us as the "hands of Jesus" to not be as effective. An easy list came up in my mind: When the church is divided, when God's people are overcome by fear and afraid to take Kingdom risks, when we are so distracted by life that we don't hear God. So I have been praying about how I might contribute to all those things and what God has to say to me about that.

This is a great experiment to have others try with you; share your photos and what stuck out to you.

Tech Fast

Depending on your personality, this could be a challenging experiment. However, it can also be very rewarding and teach you a lot! The hope for this experiment is that it will change your perspective on the way that you engage with technology but also bring your focus to the present physical spaces you are in.

- Choose one or multiple areas of technology to fast from for a designated period of time. Ideally a couple weeks or a month.
- If this is the first time you have done a tech fast, choose something that you feel you will realistically be able to fast from.
- Consider if there are ways you need to let others know that you will not be using that form of technology for this time frame.
- Write down on a sheet of paper all of the things that you feel your heart pulled toward that you consider wrong in the world around you. For instance, you might say that your heart goes out to those who are experiencing homelessness or people who are feeling isolated or lonely. Make a long list.
- Choose just one area you could take action on in your life during this tech fast.

- Create a way to remind yourself to pray for this specific issue in the world or your community today.
- Find one way to physically participate in making this wrong thing right. It may be signing up to serve alongside a ministry or humanitarian group. If that is not possible, it might look like collecting items that are needed by a group of people or some other tangible step.
- Don't try to find a grand gesture, merely find a small, yet intentional way to serve.

Talk with the friend who came with you or find a conversation partner and talk through what you discovered in this experiment.

One Way

This is a way to make an experiment local to the things in need of restoration in your community. When we join God in the restoration of all things, doubt typically takes on a different role in our minds and hearts. It also causes us to begin to ask new and different questions than we have in the past.

- Consider your local community—your city, town, or neighborhood.
- Write down on a sheet of paper all of the things that you feel your heart pulled toward that you consider wrong in your local community. Make a list as long

as possible. If you are having trouble making this list, find a local newspaper; as you look through it, you may notice the things that are in need of restoration.

- Consider something that you are able to join in for the next three months at least once a month.
- Don't try to find a grand gesture; merely find a small, yet intentional way to be a part of God's restoration in your community.

This is a great experiment to have others try with you! Find a conversation partner to discuss the effect this action takes on your questions and doubts.

PART 3

How to Stay Curious:
A Life of Passionate
Uncertainty

Choosing Resilience over Religion

*I would rather have questions that
can't be answered than answers
which can't be questioned.*
—Richard Feynman

"I'm not a runner." Whenever I say that, people think they need to respond with something like, "Sure you are! Didn't you do a 5K run last summer?" But here is the thing, I didn't *run* any 5Ks, I didn't *walk* them either. The best way you could describe what I was doing is jogging . . . slowly. So it would be more accurate to say, "I'm a jogger." The people who run past me while I am jogging are runners. What people don't realize is that calling myself a jogger is a great improvement for me! It's more than I could say a few years ago.

I had been an ice hockey player all the way through college, and after my career in hockey ended, my season of chronic pain began. My many injuries and concussions brought me to a place where I went to sleep in pain, woke up in pain, and lived my whole day in pain. Headaches, back pain, joint pain, stomach ulcers from too much Advil—it was all coming at me on a daily basis.

Once competitive ice hockey left my life, the motivation to keep moving through the pain did as well. Soon, the pain progressed to the point where it significantly affected my holistic well-being. Very few people around me knew that I was struggling; most people didn't realize just how bad the pain had gotten. This lasted for ten painful years.

Taking Off the Mask

My journey with chronic pain parallels in significant ways the various faith crises I have gone through in life. I went way longer than I needed to before I let people into what I was going through. I suffered alone when there were people close by who could have helped me feel less alone, even if they didn't have answers. I realized that I needed to be honest with people that I trusted and let them have a window into what I was going through. I didn't need to share it with everyone. It wasn't necessary to post it online or send an inter-office memo to everyone I was working with at the time. But I knew I needed to have people I could process with. People who I felt comfortable taking off the "I'm fine" mask in front of and showing them the anguish I was experiencing.

We tend to view wearing a mask as something negative, but we all wear them. Masks help us be functional human beings without projecting our issues onto everyone around us. But when we aren't able to take the mask off even with the people we can trust, we are then in a very unhealthy place.

As you face the doubts and questions and work to expand your perspective, it's important to figure out who you can take the mask off with, the people with whom you can honestly answer the question, "How are you, really?" These people don't have to be going through exactly what you are going through. But usually when you begin to take the mask off, you find others who have similar struggles hiding behind their own masks.

Who Are Your People?

Your inner circle of trust is a great place to start when you're ready to let people in to any struggle you are facing. However, those relationships have their limits. Friends aren't always (or often) able to be the people who can coach you through the hard steps you need to continue on your journey. Most of us need a process to help us move from where we are to where we want to be. I am encouraging you again like I did in chapter 9 to discover process-oriented relationships, whose purpose, at least for a time, is to help you move through the journey you are on and prevent you from getting stuck. Process-oriented relationships can come in many forms: mentors, counselors, pastors, guided support groups, groups with guidelines like Alcoholics Anonymous, life coaches, spiritual directors, and others. These relationships share one thing in common: their goal is not to tell you what to do and where to go but rather to be supportive, challenging, and encourage you to keep going and commit to a process of growth.

In order to work through the pain I was experiencing physically, I engaged in process-oriented relationships with a number of health-care professionals. I also had a personal trainer who helped me modify some workouts in order to begin to build back my strength. Similarly, in my spiritual and emotional life, I have had to choose process-oriented relationships to help me enter into a place of holistic well-being. My spiritual director has been key over the last decade. My therapist has helped me tackle specific experiences from my past as well as some issues I struggle with because of my family of origin.

In certain seasons, I have had coaches to help me learn new skills in my vocation and discipleship groups where I have been held accountable for listening to Jesus's voice in my life. Some of these groups/relationships come with a financial cost, and they all mean giving time that you might otherwise use elsewhere. Many people don't have the financial resources to pay for counselors and coaches. If you are one of those people, don't be discouraged! There are more and more free resources out there, especially if you are able to connect with others online.

Usually, it just takes a bit more perseverance and patience to do the extra digging. Even those who are able to invest financially often have an aversion to using their money in this way. Please consider how this investment in your well-being is really an investment in everyone around you! Your family, friends, coworkers, and faith community all benefit from the growth you will experience. I can't imagine where I'd be without these process-oriented relationships in my life!

Quick Fix versus the Long Haul

The pain was so hard to manage when I was in the thick of it. I looked for medication, supplements, or anything else that could make this problem go away. I went to a neurologist who did extensive tests on my brain just to tell me that there was nothing wrong with it. I learned that many people have chronic migraines and headaches with no known cause. I then went through a battery of different medications to see if they would help. The irony was that most of these medications listed headaches as one of the side effects. Nothing helped. I desperately wanted one of these doctors to have a quick fix for me so that I could go from zero to hero in a matter of days or weeks. What I soon realized was that I needed to commit to the long haul if I wanted to experience relief and healing and get unstuck.

As a pastor, people often come to me with their faith questions or experiences of doubt and hope that I have easy answers or quick-fix remedies for them. They want to avoid the uncomfortable process of deconstruction. I encourage them to commit to the long haul and to process-oriented relationships, but what I often hear from them is a lack of motivation to settle in for the long journey ahead. People often leave my office with more questions than they came in with. I know that's not what they were hoping for. But I know that pat answers are how many people got here in the first place. They wanted others to give them the quick fix to end their existential angst instead of the hard work of taking personal responsibility and being intentional with their faith.

In order to survive the long haul, we need to make friends with the tension. Tension is often seen as a negative word, but I think it is far from negative. In fact, tension is the only thing that causes anything to happen. Tension is what happens to the rubber of a tire when it is full of air. Tension is what tunes a guitar when you tighten and loosen the tuning pegs. Tension is what happens to your muscles when you go jogging or lift weights. Tension shouldn't get such a bad rap.

We tend to associate tension with stress, and stress has been completely demonized by our culture. Let's go back to Psychology 101 and examine the difference between *eu*stress and *dis*tress.[1] Eustress is the kind of stress that causes tension in your life that leads to motivation. It is what gives us the will to get out of bed every morning and make things happen in our lives, similar to the stress experienced by our muscles when they are being stretched to run a little farther and lift a slightly heavier weight set. That is the only way for them to grow! Day by day, the increase of stress on our muscles causes us to grow in our capacity. Someone who can barely run a mile when they first start, after a few weeks can already run two or three. The intentional stress they put on their muscles and lungs increases their capacity.

This is what had to happen for me to get through the season of intense chronic pain. I had to intentionally choose to put my body through stress in order to strengthen muscles I didn't know I had. It began to help minimize the pain. I also had to follow some long-term health regimens: making healthy eating choices and setting up appointments that would help me stay proactive with my health rather than reactive. It took almost two years, but eventually I found relief from the pain and increased well-being. The pain isn't completely gone—it never will be—but it's more than manageable now. Now I can jog and take boxing classes and actually enjoy the workout!

But here's the thing, I can't just let those two years be the long haul needed to deal with this pain. I will have to be intentional with strengthening my body and paying attention to my health for the rest of my life if I don't want to end up back in a dark and painful spot again.

Our spiritual lives are no different. When we are experiencing a dark season of wandering in the wilderness, it doesn't mean that there is no way out. However, we will have to experience some stress before we can begin to move through to the other side. The most important thing is that we give up on the quick fix, make friends with tension, and embrace the long haul. The choice to stay curious and live a life of passionate uncertainty is a lifelong quest, not a box that can be checked. It's not easy, but barely anything in life worth pursuing comes easy.

Moving through the Cycles

Our faith isn't a journey with a starting spot, a few scenic stops, and a destination where we arrive at a fully formed sense of ourselves, God, and the world. Psychologists like Jean Piaget and James Fowler have learned through their studies that humans' emotional and intellectual development is more cyclical than linear. Those who study the body say this is true of our physical bodies as well. So it only makes sense that our spiritual lives would be cyclical as well.

I referenced Hagberg and Guelich's book *The Critical Journey* as I introduced the wall metaphor in chapter 8. They discuss the various stages in detail, but let me outline them briefly:

Stage 1: the recognition of God—awe, sense of need, and experience of God.
Stage 2: the life of discipleship—learning about God with a community.
Stage 3: the productive life—using your talents and gifts to engage what God cares about.

Stage 4: the journey inward—rediscovering God and taking personal responsibility for the understanding you
have of your faith. The wall—life or faith crisis.

Stage 5: the journey outward—surrendering to God and
discovering a deep sense of calling.

Stage 6: the life of love—reflecting God's selfless love
through your life to those around you.

Each stage offers gifts, but it is possible to get caged in any
stage and find yourself stuck. This is most acute in stage 4 with
the wall, as I previously described.

These stages are cyclical, meaning you can be in each of
them multiple times throughout your life. They are numbered
in an order that matches the progression they often take, but
the reality is that everyone's life is different, and you can move
between them in any order. For instance, someone may be in
stage 4 and then move back to 3, then back to 4. This can happen when trying to avoid the wall. Someone could be in stage
5 and then have a very poignant experience with God and find
themselves in a deep version of stage 1—as if they are noticing God for the first time. Some people describe this sudden
enveloping of a stage 1 experience of faith after their first child
is born, for instance. That our faith is cyclical might frustrate
us because we prefer predictable, linear steps. But there we go
again with our attachment to certainty! It just isn't possible to
have certainty!

Jesus has been my constant companion throughout
the stages of faith, even when I was unsure about him as I

questioned everything, especially in stage 4. Jesus has been that true north when the stress of the tension has seemed overbearing. With Jesus as your companion, and with some others you have invited to help you on the journey, you can settle in for the long haul, realizing there are no boxes to check or ability to achieve in the life of faith. It's just one step at a time.

I need to engage in a number of daily practices to stay healthy and grow stronger physically, and it can often feel like I'm going through the motions. But week after week, and month after month, I can't deny that I am growing in my capacity and also my resilience to withstanding the pressure. Spiritually and emotionally, we take one step at a time, and it may feel like we are going through the motions. But we must make an important distinction. When you go through the motions of faith because you think you should or because you always have, you end up with lifeless religion. When you step intentionally into the motions that stretch you and lead you through the faith cycle, you end up with resilience. And resilience is a better companion for life than religion ever could be.

19

Deciding to Go through the Motions

*Are you tired? Worn out? Burned out
on religion? Come to me. Get away with
me and you'll recover your life. I'll show
you how to take a real rest. Walk with
me and work with me—watch how I do
it. Learn the unforced rhythms of grace.
I won't lay anything heavy or ill-fitting
on you. Keep company with me and
you'll learn to live freely and lightly.*

—Jesus

Balance is overrated. I've completely given up on the concept. I now have a personal vendetta against the people who coined the phrase *work-life balance*. Whoever you people are, I feel like you made promises to me that you couldn't keep! Balance isn't just overrated, it's unachievable. And, in my view, the self-care movement, which has grown in popularity and influence in the last few years, is also making promises it can't keep. I know this is an unpopular opinion. So many people I know have been swept up in the self-care movement and found it to be valuable.

The truth is, those who actually choose to care for who they are as a person through self-care gain much from the movement. I will always advocate for people to pursue holistic well-being. However, my observation is that what many label *self-care* is really *self-comfort* or even worse, *self-indulgence*. For example, the Netflix binges that allow us to get lost in an interesting or humorous story feel good, at least at first. There is also nothing wrong with getting engaged in a great show on Netflix, but when you're asked, "are you still watching?" after several hours, perhaps the answer should be "not anymore" and to turn it off.

Exchanging Rhythms for Balance

It's time to give up our quest for *balance* and embrace healthy *rhythms*. Rhythms in our lives can be found daily, weekly, or seasonally. At times, we work harder than normal, so perhaps the next season should be a time when we try to find more rest. Daily, what keeps you grounded and centered and helps you face the myriad of uncertainty that each day holds? This is where spiritual practices become so vital. They can be a part to your daily or weekly rhythms, giving you a place to start or end each day.

When I learned about spiritual practices or disciplines growing up, they were limited to just a few things: reading my Bible, a list of prayer requests, and potentially reading some sort of devotional book. These practices were grouped together in what my faith community called *devos* or *quiet time*. As an adult, I didn't want to do these things every day because it felt really forced and rote. I was going through the motions in a way that seemed like an obligation more than a way to become centered.

This all changed as I began to try out some of the experiments and practices I offered in part 2 of this book. I've learned that there are *so many* ways that God can be experienced! I began to pray deep prayers, going beyond the obligatory list of thank yous and requests. I still had to be intentional, and it did feel like a discipline—maintaining a deep prayer life was even sometimes stressful, but in a good way like the stress we discussed in the last chapter. But just like growing my capacity for jogging by going just a little farther each day, I began to grow in my capacity to connect with God through these new rhythms. I also gained a deeper connection with my own soul, paying attention to what was going on inside of me in a way that I hadn't before. In Hagberg and Guelich's model, stage 4 seasons of faith are referred to as "the inward journey." This stage emphasizes how important it is to be able to understand your own soul at a deeper level as you journey toward the core of who you are.

Trading the value concepts of balance and quiet times in for rhythms and practices made a huge difference in my life. These rhythms have kept me grounded throughout transition and change. Life doesn't really have seasons of transition; it's just one big transition. I think of transition metaphorically as a train that sometimes is moving slowly but other times is going full force down the side of a mountain. But the Transition Train rarely stops, if ever. Life keeps moving, and that means change and transition come with it!

By incorporating rhythms and practices into my life, I have come to the realization that the only consistent parts of my life are the rhythms I choose to participate in. Some days, they do feel just like going through the motions. But I have learned that they can be so helpful for me to stay grounded as life swirls around me. I don't need to be feeling it every day to benefit from the practice. People sometimes say, "I will get into regular rhythms when life calms down. My schedule is so crazy right now." My response is that they should connect with some rhythms and practices precisely *because* their life is so crazy right now.

Rhythms that leave space for listening and reflection create a regular space in my life to stay curious. Pausing to let my questions catch up to the fast pace of my life is always worth it.

When I can name the question on the surface of my life, I can often go deeper and discover what I sometimes call "the question beneath the question." But this ability to take the meaning beyond the surface takes time. It just so happens that time is already carved out when rhythms and practices are a part of my life regularly.

I have to be intentional about changing my practices in different seasons. Living in Minnesota, where we really do have four distinct seasons, the change in the weather is a helpful reminder to ask myself if my rhythms are working for me. I try to gauge what rhythms I need in the next season to help me stay connected with God, with my own soul, with the people in my community, and with the kingdom purposes God has led me to engage in. I now have what many call a Rule of Life: a list of my daily, weekly, monthly, and seasonal rhythms. Each season, it needs to be revised depending on the demands of life. Big changes in my life, relationships, or vocation require a larger overhaul of my Rule of Life.

Even though you may need to change up your rhythms and your practices seasonally, it is important to give things a reasonable amount to time to see the effect they have on your mind and heart. So many people try a spiritual practice for a week or two and then decide that it didn't do anything for them. Give it some time, people! Most things worth doing take time, and frankly we aren't very good at them right away.

My friend Dan is a musician and songwriter, and he says that any good song should either move you or be something you can move to. I just love that way of thinking about spiritual practices as well. Every single time you practice *lectio divina*, the daily *examen*, or a resonate walk, you may not feel moved or a desire to move. But when you look back over a few weeks or a month, what do you notice? Do you see your heart being drawn to a deeper place with God, yourself, or others? Do the practices lead you to action? To *move* in a direction toward something in your own life or toward justice or mercy in the lives of others? When you've given it time and it feels like a practice isn't something that moves you or that you can move to, it might be time to try something else.

Hearts Burning on the Road

The Gospel of Luke recounts a story about what happened after Jesus died and the disciples heard that he may have been resurrected and come back to life.[1] The disciples still doubted that this was true. They doubted, in part, because it was some of the women in their community who had come back from the empty tomb proclaiming the resurrection. At that time, they wouldn't give any credibility to the report of a couple of women. Even today, the testimony of women is often considered unreliable by men who want to see the evidence with their own eyes. And, of course, we are all like this—suspicious until we see something for ourselves.

The story in Luke describes how two of the disciples are walking along the road to a town called Emmaus. They are talking with each other about all that has happened over the past few days. I'm sure it had been an emotional roller coaster. It's no wonder they were doubting that Jesus was back. I think I would be too. Suddenly, Jesus begins to walk on the road beside them. The Scripture says they are "kept from recognizing him." I always think about how strange it is that they don't realize it's him. How often are we walking with Jesus on the road of life without realizing it? Jesus asks the disciples what they are talking about and then lets them recount the whole story of what happened to him. All the while, they don't realize that it's him they are talking to! (Jesus has a sense of humor.)

Then Jesus starts to tell them his story, the story of God, right from the beginning and on through to his death, making connections to the story of their forefathers and prophets and explaining why the Messiah needed to die. Through all this, they still don't recognize him. They get to Emmaus and invite Jesus to eat with them. Jesus grabs the bread and breaks it, just like he had done the last night before he died. And in that moment, they recognize him. Just as soon as they do—poof—Jesus disappears. The stories where Jesus disappears are some of my favorites. I imagine that Jesus sometimes did this just because he could, and for some reason that makes me love him more.

The disciples are left at the table bewildered, and they express something that has always intrigued me. They ask each other "were not our hearts burning within us while he talked with us on the road and opened the Scriptures to us?" Their hearts were burning. But they must have tried to ignore it. Because they didn't pay attention to their senses or share their inklings with each other, they missed the reality that they were having a divine encounter with the risen Jesus. How often in life do we miss encounters with Jesus or the Divine because we ignore the burning in our hearts? Or perhaps we have forgotten what it feels like to have our hearts burning within us (some might say we have become hard hearted). What if Jesus is walking the road right beside us, and we just aren't able to truly see him? How can we pay more attention to what is happening in our hearts?

I think we all know what that feels like—a little spark or curiosity that leads us to ask the question that is beginning to catch flame within us. A sense that there is something meaningful happening right now if we were to just stop and notice. But instead of fanning the flame, we hold it back even to the point of letting it go out, allowing curiosity and wonder to disappear. It's a mistake to think that we will only encounter God in spiritual practices. In fact, sometimes putting so much pressure on those quiet times leads to frustration. If we narrow our scope to seeing God only in those small moments of our lives, we can miss out on what Jesus may be pointing to out in the world.

We often live our lives on autopilot, going from place to place with our head down, not noticing all that's happening around us. But God is moving all the time, trying to get our attention, even though we often fail to recognize God on the road. This story helps me see that perhaps my eyes would be open if I were to let myself engage with the burning in my heart. Let my curiosity ask, "Why do I feel this sense of won-der, anger, confusion, love, or any other emotion that rises in me when I stop to notice the spark I feel in my heart?"

When your heart is burning on the road, or when you open the Scriptures, or when you have a meaningful encounter or conversation with someone, perhaps it's time to stop and won-der. Or if the situation doesn't allow you to pause, take that spark into a practice you have carved out intentionally in your Rule of Life. Those spaces will fan the flame of your curiosity, allowing it to burn away some of what consumes your restless mind. And those spaces will prepare you for what may be next on your journey.

As soon as Jesus disappears, the disciples get up and leave Emmaus and go to Jerusalem where the others are gathered. Before they can get the whole story out, Jesus appears right there in the room with them. Even though they had just failed to recognize Jesus with them on the road, when he appears this time, they assume he is a ghost! Seriously, Jesus and his disap-pearing and reappearing act!

Jesus asks them, "Why are you troubled, and why do doubts rise in your minds? Look at my hands and feet. It is I myself! Touch me and see; a ghost does not have flesh and bones, as you see I have." They are still in awe and have a hard time believing what they are seeing, but Luke makes it clear that Jesus "opened their minds" to help them understand.

Jesus was the one who opened their eyes to see that it was him sitting at the table with them. It was Jesus who opened their ears so they would know it was his voice. And it was Jesus who opened their minds to be able to comprehend at least some of what was happening around them. One of the prayers that I often repeat when I engage in spiritual practices is this:

> Jesus, open my eyes to see what you are doing around me, open my ears to hear your voice, open my mind to give me wisdom and discernment, and open my heart and give me courage to respond to the invitation to join you in your mission of redemption in the world.

20

Going beyond the Shadow of Doubt

Doubt is the shadow cast by faith.
—Hans Küng

"Let go and let God" may top the list of the most cringeworthy Christian clichés. And yet, I know that it points to something true. The more control I try to take of everything around me, the more out of control I feel. I wish the cliché "God helps those who help themselves" was more accurate. I'd rather be able to work harder *and* smarter and get the results I'm hoping for. While this may work in areas of sales or profit margins, it is just not going to get you anywhere when it comes to spirituality.

Jesus says to his followers, "Whoever wants to save their life will lose it, but whoever loses their life for me will find it." A little more poetic than "let go and let God," but I think that is what he is saying. We are the people who made it into a meme or a Hallmark card. He also expresses numerous times throughout the Scriptures that worrying about your life or trying to gain the whole world or seeking after all the things you think you need in life isn't going to do anything but lead you to "forfeit your own soul." We forfeit our own soul when we strive after things that will never give us what we desire or hope for. Running after answers or certainty will not give us the deep faith we're actually looking for. Doubt can cast a dark shadow over our lives, but I know we can live beyond the shadow of doubt.

Seeking and Surrender

It is possible to actively seek and follow our curiosity without being someone who is striving. When we notice ourselves striving, we are being motivated by a desire for control rather than following our curiosity. Notice within yourself when your anxiety is rising because what you are actually seeking is control. Stop and engage the curiosity in your heart; don't let it be drowned out by fear and anxiety. When you are in hot pursuit of control, it will feel like you are under a dark cloud of doubt casting an ominous shadow. When you are stepping into curiosity and wonder, you will see the sun peeking through the clouds, shedding light on what you are discovering. Warning: the shadow of doubt can be relentless; it takes intentionality to release control and surrender.

Sometimes, when I am feeling a need for control, which is very common for someone with my personality type, I actually find a place to sit or even lie down and I do a short body prayer. I ball my fists up like I am holding tightly onto something and I imagine all the things, people, situations that I wish I could control. Slowly I pray and ask God to help me let go and release the things I desire to control. (The Serenity Prayer can be helpful for this.) In some instances, I release just one finger at a time because I really don't want to surrender. But by the time I get to the point where my hands are open, what I realize is that I am now in a posture to receive.

Before, my hands were full and there was no way I could receive from God, or anyone else for that matter. In my open-hands moments, I have the ability to receive grace, compassion, or mercy from God—or even from myself (I have trouble giving myself compassion even when I desperately need it). I also have my hands open to hold on to curiosity—to let wonder lead me to places in my mind and heart where I don't feel the need to take back control.

When you are in the midst of doubt and questioning, you may need to do a surrender body prayer every few hours. I've been there, and I am sure I will be again. In the wilderness, we feel vulnerable, and we are tempted to try to take control.

Think back to the story of the people of God wandering in the wilderness. God gave them what they needed, like manna and quail for food every day. But they wanted to take more than they needed each day and store it up in their tents even though they were instructed not to. Their attempts at control just led to rotting food and maggots all up in their tents. Let's be honest: we all have some rotting, nasty, maggot aspects of life that have come from our desire for control. Yikes!

Of course, it takes effort to seek and discover, to follow your curiosity and passion. Just recognize that surrender is necessary if you want to have open hands to receive what you will find along the way. Surrender isn't standing still and not moving, it's letting God be the one to lead the way. This is what can help us move out from under the shadow that doubt so easily casts in our life.

Commitment versus Certainty

I got married a bit later in life than many in my community. Living nearly thirty-five years without a significant other helped me realize that I didn't need someone else to validate my role as part of the kingdom of God and my faith community. The pressure of the dominant culture toward marriage and having kids leads many single people to feel less than worthy in Christian community. As I formed intentional relationships with people in my community, long before I met my husband, I learned that covenant commitment is not only reserved for marriage but that I could make commitments to others when I experienced God leading me to do so. So in addition to my commitment to my husband, I have a covenant commitment with a group of women. We commit to always support each other as a group of friends that we believe God brought together.

In each of these commitments and promises, I thought I was signing up for more certainty. I can be *certain* that these women will be there for me because we have committed to each other. I can be *certain* that I will be married to my husband till death do us part. Of course, I know that people sometimes break their promises, and I can't be so proud as to assume I might never break a promise, either. But I trust in the promises I've made to and with these important people in my life. Even still, I've learned that by making these commitments, I have actually signed up for more uncertainty!

Not only do I have the uncertainty of my own life, but now I have taken on the uncertainty of others. The pain of loss, the confusion of calling, the disappointment and the bewilderment of being hurt by others. When they feel it, I feel it. But I also get to experience a depth of joy that I would never have in my life if it weren't for the commitment I have made to these dear people.

Through joys and sorrows and everything in between, the only constant is more uncertainty. When my husband has a setback, it's *our* setback. When my husband has a success it's *our* success. And vice versa. It's not that we have lost sight of the fact that we are two different people, but this is what it means for two to become one. In fact, when we were writing our wedding vows, my husband insisted that we include the line, "I give myself to you in faith and in doubt, in times of clarity and uncertainty." Commitment doesn't remove uncertainty; it brings more questions into your life.

The same holds true in my commitment to following Jesus. When Jesus says that there is a "new covenant in his blood,"[1] he is telling us that he has done what is necessary for us to have a commitment, a covenant, a promise that we can hold on to. In Jesus's time, people often solidified commitments with a "blood promise," or "cut a covenant."[2] People would kill an animal, separate the two sides of the animal, and ceremoniously walk through the severed animal. It was a way of saying "we can't go back," just like the blood of the animal can't be put back in its body. Jesus, of course, had his blood shed as the final blood promise between God and humanity. No future animals needed to be harmed or injured in this process!

So many of us feel that we have to be absolutely certain before we enter into a blood promise with Jesus. It makes sense! Any wise person would tell you to know what you are getting into when you sign a contract. A lot of headaches have come from failing to read the fine print. Curiosity in our pursuit of Jesus is a vital process—no question. However, saying yes to this commitment is not going to give you greater certainty but increase the uncertainty.

I believe that a commitment to Jesus means eternal life with God. John 3:16 was the first verse I memorized, just like all the other four-year-olds in my Sunday-school class. I take great comfort knowing God redeems even me and the broken world we live in. My faith gives me a sense of security in certain ways, for sure. That is what it means to me that Jesus is my Savior. However, the commitment to follow Jesus means that he is also my Lord, or more literally my leader. And it's that leadership part that leads to the uncertainty. When Jesus is the leader of your life, it's not about a list of moral rights and wrongs. I used to think that was true, but reality is much more complicated. Much more gray and less black and white.

Following Jesus is about actually being on his heels, asking some very different questions, and being willing to embrace the uncertainty that can come from the answers! When you agree to a covenant with God, through the blood of Jesus, you accept God's leadership. This will cause you to care about things that you never cared about before. Things that break God's heart will break yours. You will begin to see people the way God sees people. Just like the other covenants in my life, I take on the heart of God's people in a way that I can't escape now that I've made the commitment to be intertwined. I want to encourage you to commit to the person of Jesus and commit to the uncertainty that comes with following him. Take your time, and don't fake it. But don't wait until you have reached *all* the certainty you desire, because if you wait till then you'll never make the commitment. This kind of commitment is a scary proposition, but I promise you that it leads to a better way to live.

Imagine you have fallen in love with someone everyone in your life has come to love as well. You decide to commit to marriage, but it dawns on you, you only really know so much about who they are. What if they change? What if there are things you don't know that become important later? What if you got some things wrong about them? It's enough to give you cold feet and send you running from the altar. But anyone in your life who sees that you truly love your betrothed and knows there are no red flags would beg you not to run. That's because they know the damage it would do to your heart to live your life without the one you love by your side. As you walk down that aisle, you can't possibly know everything you need to know. Is there any way to know how you and your partner will change over the years? Nope. Do you have a perfect handbook on how to be a good partner to this specific person? Not really. Is it risky to commit to another being? Oh yeah. Will there be a whole new level of uncertainty that this relationship brings into your life? Yes. Is it worth it? I would say so.

Live Your Questions

You might choose any number of daily questions to guide your life: "What makes you happy?" or "What is most life giving?" or "What will bring me the most meaning?" or even "What is the most selfless way I can live for others today?" All those questions sound good to me, but I urge you to ask yourself these two questions each day: "What is God doing around me?" and "How will I respond?"

Curiosity should lead us to acknowledge that God is moving around us and is active in our world today. A naturally curious person would wonder, "What is this God up to?" The answer to that question is usually not written on a wall or spoken through a bush. Moving beyond our cynicism to wonder what God is doing around us will take intentionality. It is absolutely worth the risk to open our eyes and hearts to the movement of God.

Asking these daily grounding questions about God's activity has opened my life in incredible ways. When I pay attention, I am led into further questions and even to make huge changes in my lifestyle: to stop on the road and pick up strangers or to write this book! These two questions guide my curiosity. If you were to ask, "God, what are you saying to me?" I wonder how God may lead you and how it might impact your life. Sometimes I ask that question and go days without gaining any clarity or awareness. Other seasons, it feels like God is doing *so much* around me. This is just the normal rhythm of faith. Let your curiosity about God lead you in your life. You will have to take risks and bold courageous steps even when you are afraid. When you step into your daily life, living your questions actively, you will end up in places you never thought you'd be, but it's an adventure worth taking!

What Would Jesus Ask?

What would Jesus do? This question became very popular because of a book and some bracelets in the nineties. But I think there is a better question when it comes to the doubts and questions we face in our lives: What would Jesus ask? Jesus is the question man, not the answer man. Throughout the Gospels we see Jesus ask many deep and thought-provoking questions. If the questions were important enough for Jesus, perhaps they are questions we should consider as well!

Jesus asked his disciples, "Who do you say I am?"[3] If Jesus is to be your true north in the midst of chaos, coming back to this question may be crucial. Jesus also asked a blind man who reached out to him, "What do you want me to do for you?"[4] Now, I'm sure Jesus already knew the answer to this question. But Jesus knew it was important for the man to speak what he truly wanted from Jesus. We often hold back from telling Jesus what we want him to do for us. If we know what we want, let's tell him. Especially if it's guidance through the wilderness!

Some others worth considering:

"Can any one of you by worrying add a single hour to your life?"[5]

"Look at the birds of the air; they do not sow or reap or store away in barns, and yet your heavenly Father feeds them. Are you not much more valuable than they?"[6]

"Why do you look at the speck of sawdust in your brother's eye and pay no attention to the plank in your own eye?"[7]

"What good will it be for someone to gain the whole world, yet forfeit their soul? Or what can anyone give in exchange for their soul?"[8]

"Do you bring in a lamp to put it under a bowl or a bed? Instead, don't you put it on its stand?"[9]

"Do you still not see or understand? Are your hearts hardened? Do you have eyes but fail to see, and ears but fail to hear?"[10]

"Why do you call me, 'Lord, Lord,' and do not do what I say?"[11]

"For who is greater, the one who is at the table or the one who serves?"[12]

The questions we have about life, God, faith, the church, and the world aren't going to all be answered. My encouragement to you is that asking these questions means you can stay curious! Starting with the questions Jesus asked can help reorient us when our list of questions is getting long and daunting. Engaging the questions Jesus asked in the midst of our own, we can further our curiosity and step out into deeper purpose and meaning.

Like many others, one of my favorite narratives is the Chronicles of Narnia. Author C. S. Lewis creates a fictional parallel universe, which four young siblings accidentally enter in *The Lion, the Witch and the Wardrobe*. Within this world they encounter an allegorical God/Christ figure as a gentle, yet fierce lion named Aslan. During the siblings' second adventure in Narnia, *Prince Caspian*, one of the main characters, Lucy, is on a journey with her siblings through the forest of Narnia. She believes she glimpses Aslan through the trees and tells everyone they must try to follow him. It has been so long since anyone has encountered the great lion that no one believes her. She reluctantly goes along with them, forgoing the chance to try to pursue Aslan, who she had come to love so deeply on their previous adventure in Narnia.

The group stops for the night and makes camp, and Lewis describes what happens next:

"Lucy woke out of the deepest sleep you can imagine, with the feeling that the voice she liked best in the world had been calling her name."[13]

She begins to walk through the forest, trying to follow the sound of her name. She finally steps into a clearing, and there is Aslan sitting in the moonlight. She can't contain herself, and she throws her arms around him in the sheer joy of seeing him tangibly before her.

"Welcome, child," he said.

"Aslan," said Lucy, "you're bigger."

"That is because you are older, little one," answered he.

"Not because you are?"

"I am not. But every year you grow, you will find me bigger."[14]

The expansion that happens in our life causes us to grow. Contrary to what we, and Lucy, might think, it doesn't cause our experience of God to shrink. It usually causes it to expand. We may experience wandering through the woods trying to find God in the midst of the wilderness. We may go a long while not hearing anything at all. But when something familiar seems to call your name, don't let anyone or anything hold you back from following after its sound. When wonder moves us to follow what might be God, there are seasons where we come to a clearing and encounter Jesus in a way that seems different from our previous experience. And when we do, there is a good chance we will have grown. So when we come upon him, we will find him bigger than we ever had before.

FINAL THOUGHTS:
LIVING A CURIOUS LIFE

Curiosity is making a comeback. My little nephew loves Curious George, the little monkey that I remember from when I was a kid. The fun stories about George and the Man with the Yellow Hat help him embrace a healthy and good form of curiosity.

Curiosity has cured viruses and diseases. Curiosity has given us amazing things like vaccines, airplanes, iPhones, and Silly Putty. Curiosity helped us discover the world is round and helped us to land a human on the moon. Curiosity gives young people the courage to ask someone out on their first date, and curiosity gives us the intrigue needed to try to figure out the needs of our kids, all of whom are very different.

Curiosity has offered all these things to the world, and yes, it has brought some danger and risk. Like anything in life, it can lead to good and evil, blessings and curses, and everything in between. But what curiosity leads to, more than anything else, is a *deeper* sense of curiosity. Awe, wonder, and mystery are fueled by curiosity. Curiosity isn't safe, but hopefully now you can see that it's good.

Curiosity has saved my faith more than once, and curiosity has changed my life in ways that fill me with gratitude. If you make the commitment to stay curious in your life, you will arrive at *some* of the answers you seek. But there is no doubt that you will also arrive at deeper questions. For that you can be thankful, because sometimes what we *want* in life are more answers but what we really *need* are better questions. So stay curious my friends, because God is found in the questions, not only in the answers.

Access the *Stay Curious* podcast, additional resources for small groups, and deeper study at: PastorSteph.com/StayCurious.

OATH OF CURIOSITY

I swear to fulfill, to the best of my ability and judgment, this oath:

I will be brave and courageous and choose curiosity over comfort.

Where I'm tempted to wander, I will choose to follow wonder.

Letting go of certainty, I will embrace the mystery of God.

I will notice when I am being a skeptic and choose to be a seeker.

I will assume God is bigger than my human mind can fully comprehend.

I will go through the wall brick by brick and not ignore it.

When I feel my heart and mind expanding, I'll accept that although it's painful, it is good.

I will be honest about my doubts, even if it's hard to admit I have them.

I will check my baggage for stowaways.

I will slay my dragons of fear, grief, and anger, as different seasons bring new dragons.

I will reject dualistic thinking and the idea that there are only two forks in the road.

In my relationships, I will seek to understand the nuance of different perspectives.

I will encourage others to discover and embrace their questions.

I will stay open to what I can learn from those who are different from me.

When I feel stuck, I will try experiments that help me keep moving.

I will make friends with the tension.

I will choose resilience over religion.

I will only go through the motions if I am going through them on purpose.

I will go beyond the shadow that doubt so easily casts.

I will choose to live into the questions that really matter to me.

I will choose passionate uncertainty.

I will choose to stay curious—and thus become more fully alive.

ACKNOWLEDGMENTS

Thank you to the many people who helped me make my first book a reality: My family, including my husband, JD, for being my biggest cheerleaders; my other encouragers—Jo, Nicole, Michael, D1:9 and BALP Ladies, and my Mill City Church team and community. Thank you to my agent, Rachelle; my editor, Lisa; and the team at Fortress Press. Thank you to Christine for offering me a beautiful space to write as well as helping me come up with all those experiments based on your extensive experience with this topic. To Steve, for the generosity of time and advice that helped this pastor become a writer. Thank you to my spiritual director, Jean—you walking with me for these last eleven years has meant more than I can say. To my therapist Jeff—we really should start a therapist appreciation day for you all and the incredible work you do! To Claire for being my sister/coach and letting me be the same for you. For those who I know personally whose story or work I referenced in this book: Rod, Amos, Claire, James, Siri, Dan, Greg, Alan, Janet, Stefan, JD, Sarah, Jonathan, Graham, Daniel, and Aslan—I know you're a fictional lion but you seem so very real to me.

NOTES

Chapter 2

1. Google Dictionary, s.v. "catechism."
2. Mark 12:1.
3. John 3:1–15.
4. John 4:1–30.
5. Mark 4:11–12.
6. Revelation 3:15–16.

Chapter 4

1. Letter to Rev. Joseph Neuner, 1961.
2. Genesis 28:10–22.
3. Genesis 32:22–32.
4. Exodus 3.
5. Exodus 13:20–22.
6. Luke 2:36–38.
7. John 5:19–20.
8. Acts 2.
9. Acts 10, Acts 16.
10. Acts 16:7.
11. Acts 15:28.

Chapter 5

1. Ana-Maria Rizzuto, *The Birth of the Living God: A Psychoanalytic Study* (Chicago: University of Chicago Press, 1979).
2. Rizzuto, *Birth of the Living God*, 109.
3. This is a very brief description of the atonement, or what Jesus accomplished on the cross. Volumes have been written on the breadth of how powerful Jesus's resurrection was for humanity. One of my favorites is Scot McKnight, *A Community Called Atonement* (Nashville: Abingdon, 2007).
4. "Glossary: Wesleyan Quadrilateral, The," United Methodist Church, https://tinyurl.com/ybkr2fgx, quoted from Alan K. Waltz, *A Dictionary for United Methodists* (Nashville: Abingdon, 1991).
5. https://theglobalchurchproject.com/

Chapter 6

1. Joan Chittister, *Called to Question* (Lanham, MD: Sheed & Ward, 2004), 29.
2. Randy Peterman, "Theological Reductionism," *Randy Peterman Dot Com* (blog), November 8, 2006, http://tinyurl.com/ybgp8y4x.
3. Ephesians 3:14–21.

Chapter 7

1. Daniel Taylor, *The Myth of Certainty: The Reflective Christian and the Risk of Commitment* (Downers Grove, IL: InterVarsity, 1999), 80.
2. Taylor, *Myth of Certainty*, 81.
3. Gregory A. Boyd, *The Benefit of the Doubt: Breaking the Idol of Certainty* (Grand Rapids: Baker, 2013), 15.
4. National Study of Youth and Religion, Notre Dame, https://youthandreligion.nd.edu.

5. Christian Smith and Melina Lundquist Denton, *Soul Searching: The Religious and Spiritual Lives of American Teenagers* (Oxford: Oxford University Press, 2005), 162.
6. John 3:1–21.
7. Taylor, *Myth of Certainty*, 153.
8. Martin Luther King Jr., *A Gift of Love: Sermons from Strength to Love and Other Preachings* (Boston: Beacon, 2012), 115.

Chapter 8

1. Janet O. Hagberg and Robert A. Guelich, *The Critical Journey: Stages in the Life of Faith* (Salem, WI: Sheffield, 2005), 97.
2. Romans 5:3–5 *The Message* translation.
3. Lorna Collier, "Growth after Trauma," *Monitor on Psychology* 47, no. 10 (November 2016): 48.
4. Richard G. Tedeschi and Lawrence G. Calhoun, "The Post Traumatic Growth Inventory: Measuring the Positive Legacy of Trauma," *Journal of Traumatic Stress* 9, no. 3 (1996): 455–71, doi.org/10.1002/jts.2490090305.

Chapter 9

1. John Carpenter, "Boston Beer Company's Jim Koch on the Crucial Difference between Dangerous and Merely Scary," *Forbes*, May 31, 2016, https://tinyurl.com/y7xnjfyw.
2. Thank you to Dr. Christine Osgood, LMFT DMin, for helping me develop the experiments in part 2.

Chapter 10

1. Genesis 32:22–32.
2. Matthew 14:29–30.
3. John 20:24–29.
4. "Two-Thirds of Christians Face Doubt," Barna, July 25, 2017, https://tinyurl.com/ycpj9d2b.
5. A hermeneutic is the lens through which you are approaching a specific passage. In this chapter, you can hear that I am assuming

a hermeneutic that takes all of the Bible into account when trying to decide the meaning of a specific text for today.

6. Jude 9.

7. Exegesis: discovering the original, intended meaning of a given text through careful, systematic study. Exegesis is an effort at reaching back into history to the original author and audience.

8. Jeremiah 29:13.

9. Psalm 95:8, Proverbs 28:14, Zechariah 7:12.

10. Acts 17:24–28.

11. See also Henri J. M. Nouwen, *The Return of the Prodigal Son: A Story of Homecoming* (New York: Doubleday, 1994).

12. Adapted from F. LeRon Shults and Steven J. Sandage, *Transforming Spirituality: Integrating Theology and Psychology* (Grand Rapids: Baker Academic, 2006).

Chapter 11

1. James H. Cone, *The Cross and the Lynching Tree* (Maryknoll, NY: Orbis, 2011), loc. 3059 of 4753, Kindle.

2. From an interview quoted in Ian Punnett, *How to Pray When You're Pissed at God* (New York: Harmony, 2013), 10.

3. Jonathan Martin, *How to Survive a Shipwreck: Help Is on the Way and Love Is Already Here* (Grand Rapids: Zondervan, 2016), 195.

Chapter 12

1. Psalm 139:7–8.

Chapter 13

1. Peter Scazzero, *Emotionally Healthy Spirituality* (Nashville: Thomas Nelson, 2006), 124–25.

2. This concept of grief as the antidote to denial is from Walter Brueggemann, *Reality, Grief, Hope: Three Urgent Prophetic Tasks* (Grand Rapids: Eerdmans, 2014).

3. "American Say They Are More Anxious Than a Year Ago; Baby Boomers Report Greatest Increase in Anxiety," American

Psychiatric Association, May 7, 2018, https://tinyurl.com/y75wxxrq.
4. Ian Punnett, *How to Pray When You're Pissed at God* (New York: Harmony, 2013), 28.

Chapter 14

1. Matthew 12:48–50.

Chapter 15

1. Jack Abramowitz, "443. Sewing the Sheets of Parchment," Orthodox Union, https://tinyurl.com/ybnlvfp3.
2. Ian Punnett, *How to Pray When You're Pissed at God* (New York: Harmony, 2013), 29.
3. Hebrews 4:12.
4. John 16:12–13a.

Chapter 16

1. This theological interpretation of the purpose of the church is widespread and typically referred to as *missional theology*. Many scholars have been influential in shaping this understanding of the church, but Lesslie Newbigin is one of the core missiologists who started the reframe that has led to the current conversation.

Chapter 17

1. Stephanie Petit, "Louis C. K. and *SNL* Take on Liberal Internet 'Activists' in a Hilarious Music Video," *People*, April 9, 2017, https://tinyurl.com/y92g89lx.
2. Jack Alexander, "Barna and Author Jack Alexander Discover a Compromised View of Mercy," Cision, July 18, 2018, https://tinyurl.com/y7hvroym.
3. "Does Mercy Influence Christians' Actions?" Barna, August 28, 2018, https://tinyurl.com/y9khu8lo.

4. Xavier Devictor and Quy-Toan Do, "How Many Years Do Refugees Stay in Exile?" *Development for Peace* (blog), The World Bank, September 15, 2016, https://tinyurl.com/ybs834xb.
5. "Our Story," One2One, one2onementor.org/about-us.html.

Chapter 18

1. For a very interesting read, or TED Talk for that matter, check out Kelly McGonigal, *The Upside of Stress* (New York: Avery, 2015).

Chapter 19

1. Luke 24:13–35.

Chapter 20

1. 1 Corinthians 11:25.
2. Genesis 15:1–21, Jeremiah 34:18–20.
3. Matthew 16:15.
4. Mark 10:51.
5. Matthew 6:27.
6. Matthew 6:26.
7. Matthew 7:3.
8. Matthew 16:26.
9. Mark 4:21.
10. Mark 8:17–18.
11. Luke 6:46.
12. Luke 22:27.
13. C. S. Lewis, *Prince Caspian* (New York: Macmillan, 1951), 113.
14. Lewis, *Prince Caspian*, 117.